Finding My Sacred

JOURNEY OF THE SOUL

Shell Silversmith

"Anxiety is part of my life experience, it doesn't define me, nor does it have to be a life sentence."

Idea Creations Press
www.ideacreationspress.com

Copyright © 2022 by Shell Silversmith.

All rights reserved.

Published in the United States by Idea Creations Press LLC.

LIBRARY OF CONGRESS CATALOGING-IN-PUBLICATION DATA
Names: Silversmith, Shell, author
Title: Finding My Sacred: A Soul Journey / Shell Silversmith
Description: First edition. | Salt Lake City: Idea Creations Press, 2022.
Identifiers: LCCN 2022916411
ISBN 978-1948804295 (hardcover) 9781948804288 (paperback)
Subject: Autobiography | spiritual journey | life journey | spiritual awakening | healing of the soul

www.ideacreationspress.com

Cover design by Habibilah Ayoola
Interior book design by Douglas L Jones
Edited by Kristin Waller
Author Photo by Samuel Gonzalez Photography

For Richard Nelson Smith and Ida B Smith

Finding My Sacred

Contents

My Sin 1
Grandpa's Hands 6
My Family 9
Becoming Silent 12
Into Darkness (1987) 25
Angel Appears 36
Dream Man 41
Losing Faith 51
Last Moments 59
Like a Snowflake 69
Baby Bliss 70
Darkness of Addiction 74
Addiction 76
Losing Me 87
Dream Premonition 106
Car Accident 109
Agoraphobia 116
Grandma Sue 121
Hospital Visit 127
The Release 131
Discarding Noise 144

The Shift	150
The Mind	153
My Intuition	154
Aha Moment	158
Quantum Healer	166
Self-Reflection	171
Self-Discovery	178
In Poverty	184
My Gift	191
Self-Acceptance	196
Fears	202
Energy & Frequency	208
Visualization	215
Moving Forward	219
Spiritual Connection	228
Power	234
The Shift	236
Indianapolis 500	243
Authentic Self	251
Finding My Sacred	255
Acknowledgements	267

My Sin

At the church, the sky looked sullen, dark, and eerie. I was headed to confess my unholiness to the new visiting priest at the Catholic church I attended. He was a new face to the parish from South America, who arrived here three months ago. When I initially met him, he gave me his phone number; after that, we frequently prayed together.

At one of our meetings, he hypnotically gazed into my eyes as if looking into my soul. His white teeth gleamed against his tanned brown skin. He had a slight goatee and a balding head. I couldn't shake the feeling that something was amiss. I tried to convince myself otherwise. I had to trust him; maybe he could settle my mind and put my soul at ease. He was a man of God.

He wore the cloth. I hoped he wasn't too shocked at what I was about to confess. He had presided over many confessions; mine could not be the worst. I imagined being told to do a lot of Hail Mary and Our Father prayers. I wanted to be forgiven, to be in God's favor again. I hoped that all the mental pain that had transferred into physical pain would be released from my body.

I looked at the shiny floor. The fumes from the bleach made my eyes water. The chapel was immaculately clean, all polished for the good people of the faith, not for sinners like me. My fingers unconsciously dipped themselves into the holy water as I made the sign of the cross which was now a second nature gesture. The place was in semi-darkness, giving it a gloomy vibe. It was briskly cool; my hands were cold, yet damp. I kept fiddling with my hands because I was nervous.

It was winter, mid-December, and for some reason, I imagined this was what the final day on death row would be like. I walked into the partially lit hallway and paced back and forth in front of a pew. My mouth was dry as panic crept in, and I struggled to swallow. My mind told me this was a huge mistake. There was a water fountain in the foyer. I gulped down the water, and I was able to swallow again. My body wanted to run outside and race to the comfort and safety of my home. I felt shame, despair, and dread. I needed to be here; I was tired of running away from difficult situations.

I'd rather die here than be a coward, I told myself.

I heard rustling footsteps from behind the gated iron door. Father Gustavo appeared, opened it, and invited me in with a faint smile. The gate slammed behind us, and I thought of death row again. He escorted me into the confession booth, which was tiny, suffocating, and almost completely dark inside; however, the chair was soft and comfortable. I sat down and heard him seat himself from behind the curtain. The directions were written on a piece of paper in front of me.

"You may proceed," he said. I made the sign of the cross.

"Bless me, Father, for I have sinned; my last confession was two years ago, please forgive me." I paused.

"Father, I committed a sin. I…I once had an abortion." I whispered.

There was a sudden thunderous thud of a Bible being slammed from the other side of the curtain; it startled me.

"You committed a mortal grave sin!" he scolded me.

I feared for my life and sprinted out of the confession booth. I flung open the white pearly gate, which slammed shut behind me. My heart raced; my mind was confused and guilt-ridden. I fumbled for my keys and hastily opened the car door. It felt like I was running away from the grim reaper. I envisioned him in his black robe, carrying a scythe and hammering me with it.

I glanced at the entrance to the church. Nothing.

I drove to my house; my phone pinged loudly. It was a text message from Father Gustavo.

It read, **"YOU'RE GOING TO HELL! YOU'RE GOING TO HELL!"**

It was written repeatedly, over and over again in bold text.

Grandpa's Hands

I am four years old. My room is enveloped in pitch darkness. Light footsteps awaken me as I sense the presence of an older gentleman. He scoops me up from my bed. I cannot see well at first, but then my tiny eyes adjust. I see a shadow of a cowboy hat. To me, it's my grandfather Shank Tsosie, my *shicheii*, which in Navajo means my *grandpa (maternal)*. His arms are solid and bold, his scent is like a cozy Pendleton blanket. It reminded me of the meeting we had a few months ago, when he was alive.

There's a sparkly flash emitting from his belt buckle. It feels natural to be reacquainted with him again. I lay my head on his soft lumberjack shirt. He is home. In our very last meeting, he picked me up from the back of his pickup truck. It was the carefree season of summer; we attended a family picnic in Arizona. We shared a bottle of glistening strawberry soda and ate gumdrops together.

Grandpa is in one of my earliest memories. When I was three years old, I was sitting with my mom and dad in a sweat lodge. He sang with the medicine man as the reflection of the fire flickered on our faces.

As he held me, time ceased to exist. All was okay, and nothing could ever harm either of us.

My grandfather was a bold leader who spoke his mind. That night, we walked around the house in a timeless realm. When we entered the kitchen, the floor squeaked, as it usually did. He carried me through the living room. I glanced at the mirror on the wall and saw our shadowy figures. He finally, gently laid me down in my bed and abruptly disappeared.

I felt a longing for him; I wanted him to come back. Then I fell into a slumber.

At the time of this brief encounter, this was a real event; we were in between the spirit world and the earthly world. He was a being that had crossed over and had chosen to come back to say his goodbye to me. I might have been taken to his realm, which could explain some of my clairvoyant abilities. I theorize that when I saw him lifeless at the funeral, he knew how confused I was. He returned to give me a sense of closure, a sense of *yes, I still live on. I am still in existence. You were right.*

My Family

My mom and dad, Richard and Ida Smith, both of Navajo descent, met at Intermountain Indian Boarding School in Brigham City, Utah. My father excelled at automotive skills, and as a boy, he was always taking objects apart and putting them back together.

My mother, Ida, was a student body officer, on the swim team, and had her eyes set on nursing. My father eventually became a welder who worked twelve-hour shifts. He had a timely sense of humor, kind eyes, and a quiet demeanor. My earliest memories were of him calling me his "little gal." If I ran and skinned my knees, he was the first to swoop me up in his arms and ask if I was okay. My mother, on the other hand, would scold me for running. She was more worried about the hole I had made in my leggings. A fiery lady with a will of steel, she was the head of the household and a no-nonsense, intelligent, strict woman who commanded respect. My parents adopted my younger brother and I, both of Navajo descent, from birth. It wasn't an issue for me; my extended family was all I knew.

I found my passion in the first grade when my teacher, Mrs. Bainter, would read us part of a novel daily. Books sparked my imagination and interest. Once she read *The Pearl*, by John Steinbeck. As she read, I could imagine the vivid scenery, smell the scents, and feel the same feelings as the characters. I knew I had to experience more of these wonderful stories. I always looked forward to reading time.

The first book I remember reading was a

book about horses called *Take Care of Dexter*. I remember the essence of the book, not so much each word. It described a girl's love for a horse. The story touched me. The next book I remember reading was *The Count of Monte Cristo*, a classic. For the average first grader, it was a challenging book; for me, it was effortless. I can't say I understood everything, but I had the premise and a dictionary. I remember the feeling it left me, the impression. I loved losing myself in another character.

From that point on, I threw myself inwardly into the world of books. Always one to prefer classic novels to the current mainstream ones, my all-time favorite novel has become Hermann Hesse's *Siddhartha*. Siddhartha made egotistical mistakes and was still able to redeem himself. It's where I remember the words, the story, and most of all—the journey.

Becoming Silent

Being raised by an emotionally strong and independent woman was both a blessing and a curse for me. My mother was forced as a child to attend a boarding school miles away from her family. As a means of survival, she had to be responsible. She told me about the school she attended on the reservation and the expectations the school had of its students. She described the horrors of kids being slapped for talking in Navajo and how she told herself, "I'll run away if they do that to me."

On one occasion, the teacher gave my mom a sponge and bucket—she was ten years old—and told her to scrub the toilets with feces on them and to scrub the dirty floor. She refused to do it and sent a message for her dad to come to the boarding school. My grandfather rode his horse to the school and demanded to talk to the person in charge. He pulled his daughter from the school, then threatened to take the administration in front of the tribal council. He told the director that if he heard they were still mistreating their students, he would find a way to shut them down.

As an adolescent, my mother ended up attending a school in Brigham City, Utah. Expectations of herself were high. She would volunteer for school functions and oversee many school projects, all while working as a nurse's aide. Later, when she had her own family, she dressed us all nicely for church, and we drove across town to a large Presbyterian church on Sundays. She always wore lipstick and heels, and her purses always matched her shoes; pure elegance.

"There are two qualities people immediately notice when they look at you," she would tell me. "Your teeth and shoes." Keep your shoes and teeth clean, she would lecture to me. She was the one who volunteered for the P.T.A. at school. She became the treasurer in bowling, someone true to her word, a meticulous Virgo. She surrounded herself with similar people, through bowling, church, and within the neighborhood.

In the Navajo community, introducing yourself by your mother and father's clan is important.

My mother's clan is *Kinłichíi'nii*, the 'Red House People,' and my father's clan is *Tó'aheedlíinii*, the 'Water Flows Together.'

In the summer my skin was brown; in the winter, a pale brown. I loved my skin color, I loved my white teeth, and I loved my oversized cheeks, even though Tom Diggins in the fifth grade told the other boys, "She's average looking; if she put on makeup, she would be cute."

I looked at him and said, "You're average looking, too, but you can't do anything about it, can you?"

The other kids laughed. Kids liked me when I was funny. Being the class clown, everyone liked me, except for the teacher. I tried that out for a year and then became a serious student.

My mom would put me in dresses and braid my hair every morning for school. She would tell me to act like a lady. Finally, I won out, and she quit putting me in dresses. Dad gave in and bought me dump trucks, a Big Wheel, a glove, and a bat.

My father Richard lost his mom when he was fourteen years old. He, his older brother, and his mom were crossing a ditch in New Mexico. A sudden burst of water came out of nowhere, and my father and uncle were able to make it to the shore. His mother was washed away by the tide. From that point on, my grandfather relied a lot on the Catholic church to help him educate his young children. The youngest child was two years old. My father never talked to me about this experience, but there was a sadness in his eyes that I believe was there because of the challenging experience he had as a teenager.

My mother put me in ice skating and piano lessons. I hated going. I carried a Rubik's cube around with me and played the song "Jessie's Girl" on my Walkman. This I understood. I could solve all the cube but not the top layer. After much persuasion, my mom let me play on a softball team. I ended up quitting when the coach was treating me different.

I was late one day, and she refused to let me play in the game. Yet the week before, another girl was late; she happened to be

Caucasian, and she was able to play. My mother gave the coach a piece of her mind and told the lady she'd better refund our money, or she would have something coming, and the lady refunded our money.

On the car ride home, my mom told me never to let anyone treat me with disrespect. She told me because I was Navajo, some people may not like the color of my skin, or they may think I'm uneducated. She told me to always prove them wrong. I loved playing basketball; I was on the team in junior high and was disappointed when I didn't make my high school team. I went straight to the coach after missing the tryouts.

"You scored, your shot is accurate, but you're a horrible passer when you decide to pass the ball. Try again next year," he said.

That put a chip on my shoulder for the whole year, but I kept playing anytime I could with the guys. My specialty was shooting free throws. I'd be in the backyard and shoot free throws until the sun went down; it helped clear my mind. Basketball was replaced by soccer; my dream position was acquired as a starting center forward.

My mom did everything in her mind that she thought was right. Even pushing me academically. I would win contests and come in third or fourth, and she would tell me, now if you work harder, you can be first. In my mind, I heard, *You're not good enough.*

I get why she was like that. When she was fourteen years old, she was a whole state away in boarding school. If she happened to leave her coat somewhere on an outing, she wasn't going to get a replacement. Her mom wasn't going to show up with another coat because she was hundreds of miles away. My mother had to be responsible and think on her toes because she was literally on her own, and she expected me to be responsible too.

There were numerous times, if I wasn't ready, she would leave me. I would be late getting ready, and she would be gone. If I missed the bus during my freshman year in high school, she would tell me to have fun walking. I hated her at times for being cold. Yet, it instilled within me the need to be on time. Sometimes she would slap my face or hit my hand. Secretly in my little mind, I wondered if I had been her biological child if she would have hit me.

Her punishments were extreme, but they pushed me to master the art of deception. At the age of sixteen, my first boyfriend Jason and I were making out at the park. I waltzed into the house past my curfew. There was a pile of clothes waiting to be ironed. I was told I could only go to bed once everything was ironed and hung up. Three hours later, I was down to her blouse. I was so tired that I ended up leaving the iron on a piece of clothing for too long, and it burned a hole through her favorite top! Luckily, I didn't burn the ironing board.

The next day, I went to three different department stores with her blouse, asking every sales lady, "Where can I find this frilly thing?" Finally, I found a Sears department store with the same blouse. I purchased it, took the tags off, and hung it in her closet as if I'd just ended a covert military operation. She never knew! This experience taught me that there were always infinite amounts of possibilities in any situation. I developed a *never give up, I can find a way* attitude.

I was anything but a little lady—more like a little daredevil. When the neighbor boy took my little brother Darrick's Big Wheel, I marched into my dad's garage, pulled out a two-by-four, and was bound to get the Big Wheel back. The boy gave the Big Wheel back and crawled up a tree. Unbeknownst to me, my mother proudly watched the incident from the living room window. Incidentally, in high school, the boy I chased up the tree, I ended up going to prom with.

I remember my mom countlessly telling me to be quiet. When I misbehaved, she would smack me out of nowhere. She didn't do it in malice; it was what she was shown and what was expected of her generation. To obey and be silent.

Another factor that contributed to my quiet demeanor was an instance of sexual abuse, which my parents never educated me about. In the 1970s, society was very hush-hush about the taboo subject.

I was an eight-year-old, and my mom and dad had hired a first-time babysitter across the street. All I remember is her name was Tasia. She was a lanky sixteen-year-old girl with long brown hair, nothing out of the ordinary. My mom and dad went out, my brother fell asleep early, and I was watching television with the sitter. I was lying on my stomach in front of the television set with an extra-large coloring book. I had my favorite sky-blue crayon in my hand and was coloring a page. I was thirsty and went to the kitchen to get some orange juice.

When I came back into the living room, my babysitter was laying nude on the couch. On display were her little, perky boobs and a small patch of hair on her crotch. My little mind was confused and shocked! I knew this was something out of the ordinary. I literally froze in place; my orange juice slipped to the floor and splashed.

She told me she would tell my mom and dad I was being bad, and that I had purposely spilled orange juice on the floor. She wanted me to touch her private area, and then she would tell my mom and dad that I was a good girl. I turned around, ran to the bathroom as fast as possible, and locked the door.

The girl knocked on the door, telling me how sorry she was and that I was going to be in trouble if I didn't open the door. I stayed in there for what felt like an hour until I heard my mom and dad pounding on the door. The sitter was outside having a cigarette, and she'd locked herself out of the house. My mom said she wasn't paying her, and she would never come to babysit again.

I never told my mom or dad about that incident. I never spoke of it until a recent counseling session.

After the incident, I had trouble being alone in a room with anyone other than my parents. I hated orange juice for a while because it would subconsciously trigger the confusing memory. I was perplexed; I wondered why did she do that to me? I interpreted the incident as a personal attack directed toward me. A part of me felt shame, and another part wanted to bury the memory away. I also preferred the company of male energy. I would hang out with my boy cousins, especially my uncles.

Being silent allowed me to develop listening skills; however, joining a group discussion in junior high school was intimidating. My silent, observant demeanor followed me throughout young adulthood. I discovered the world would knock you down and there was no place for a silent voice. If I'd found my voice earlier, I would have thrived in the workplace. Instead, I thrived intuitively. I was able to feel, think, decipher body language, and feel energies. I could now walk into a room and walk right up to a person in emotional or physical pain and start small talk with them, even if the person was a stranger. I found myself wanting to heal others and free them from their pain. Silence brought me these gifts.

Into Darkness (1987)

In my belief system, I believe there are many realms, meaning other complete worlds that exist. There are three that are meaningful to me. The first is the earthly realm, where humans and animals reside, where time is overbearing and always dictating our lives. Then there is a realm where the spirit world and earthly world co-exist. I call this the spirit world; it's timeless. Lastly, there is the heavenly realm where angels, spirits, and the Creator exist in unison.

When I was sixteen and had begun to drive, it was a crisp fall. That's when the terrible dreams started happening.

I couldn't remember the details, but I knew there was an unsettled heaviness that surrounded me. A black cloud descended upon my surroundings, which tainted me with despair and isolation. This was my first encounter with anxiety. I was doing well with a job, a car, and good grades, yet I was out of balance.

I was angry, and I would argue with my parents. I remember one dispute that was strange. I came home at 1:00 a.m., which was past curfew. I told them the truth, that I had lost track of time while talking to friends at the mall, and they scolded me. It angered me! I could have lied to them and told them I was at a pottery class or busy doing homework at a friend's house. Instead, I was honest with them, and in a moment of anger, I yelled at them, slammed the door, and wandered out into the darkness for an hour.

On my way home, when I was five houses away from my house, I glimpsed a figure coming toward me. At that same moment, my mom and dad appeared in their car. They had been looking for me. The figure was hunched and cloaked in black. It wore a hood and walked slowly. I glanced up at it as my parent's headlights beamed on me and the shadowy figure. The face looked like that of a witch, which startled me! I fearfully ran to my mom and dad's car.

"Who was that?" my mom questioned.

Fearing for our safety, I told her I didn't know and begged my parents to hurry up and take us home. I was puzzled as to who would be running around in the darkness in a costume. Were they trying to scare me? If that was their purpose, it worked. At the time, I brushed it off as a mentally disturbed person out to scare people. Now as I look back, it seems to fit in the realm of witchcraft or shadow people. A realm that I don't want to encounter again, which to me exists and has its good and bad forces within it.

For a week after this experience, I would wake up in a sweat, feeling frazzled for the rest of the day. One night, I awoke and quickly turned my bedroom lights on. I saw my dad bent over putting something in my shoes. I asked him what he was doing. He said he'd had a bad dream about me and my car. He told me he was sprinkling corn pollen from his medicine bag into my shoes and on top of my car to protect me. I thanked him, but in the back of my mind, I thought it was a strange thing to do. How could yellow sprinkles in a bag help me?

The next day, he gave me a medicine bag, and we went outside. He told me a prayer to repeat and explained that the medicine bag was powerful and sacred. He directed me to always sprinkle to the east first because that is the starting point of life, that is where the sun begins to rise, where all directions begin. Then he sprinkled it toward the other three directions. He taught me the significance of the number four.

There are four directions, four seasons, and four elements; from that point on, I loved the number four. He told me anytime I felt unsafe to ask the Creator for protection and guidance. I agreed (with a little reluctance). I was still skeptical about having this little bag for protection, yet I trusted my dad.

My dad was into more traditional teachings than my mom. He told me about sage and how to light it and how to say a prayer. He told me about medicine men and how they sang with prayers and blessed each part of the body. I learned about snow bathing and how it was good for the circulatory system and how it prepares you for the hardships in life.

I half-listened; after all, I was growing up trying to fit in with my Anglo counterparts. The last thing I needed as a teen was to be different from everyone else.

I began to carry my medicine bag with me everywhere I went.

The next night, I awoke in fear upon hearing a large gathering of crows screeching outside. They were squawking loudly and banging against my window. I listened to see if this noise awoke anyone else in the household. I pinched myself to figure out if I was dreaming. I wasn't. I peeked into my brother's room, called his name, and heard him sound asleep. Nobody in my house was stirring. I carefully took out my medicine bag and held it to my heart, which was pounding hard, then quickly walked outside toward the squealing crows.

The wind had picked up, and the chain to the tetherball pole began to clank loudly, along with the shrieking birds. What was wrong with them? What made my heart race, even more, was the sound of a swarm of bees somewhere nearby. I nervously took out my medicine bag and did the prayer my dad had taught me. I swear, as soon as I finished the prayer, I felt a sudden gust of wind blow through, then everything was silent.

The flock of birds flew away, the wind subsided, the bees went silent, and the clanking stopped. It was as though I was pulled into another dimension and whisked back to reality. I took a deep breath and returned to a sense of peace and well-being. My dad was right, he knew how to protect me, I would never doubt his words again. I scurried back to bed and was able to get a good night's rest.

The next day was a Saturday. I remember it well. I had to work until closing at the hot dog and lemonade stand. We stayed open an hour later than usual. I worked with my friend and co-worker, blonde spike-haired Brad. We did the extra prep for the next morning and stayed open later to accommodate a big weekend crowd. We left the store around 11:00 p.m. He walked me to my car, and I embarked on my drive home in my blue Camaro with a nagging sense that I needed to drive slowly. It was a memory that I would never forget. I was eight minutes into my drive, halfway home when I approached a green light. Suddenly, a loud inner voice screamed in my head, "Stop!"

I glanced at my rearview mirror to see if anyone was behind me but saw no one. My Camaro was at a crawling pace as I drew closer to the green light. Within an instant, a lifted black pickup truck zoomed through a red light. If I was driving at normal speed, the truck would have hit me on my side of the door—it would have been deadly! A second later the light turned yellow, then red. I couldn't believe what had happened! It felt like the longest red light of my life. The red reflection lit up the inside of my car, as all the what-ifs raced through my head. My poor parents, I hadn't accomplished anything yet.

What had just happened? That asshole! Was he drunk?

Finally, the light turned green. I could go home in peace.

"That was it!" I exclaimed.

Then the thought, "It's not my time," came to mind. The realization that I was almost hit at sixty mph from the driver's side devastated me.

From that moment on, I told myself, "You must listen to your intuition, listen to that inner voice."

Up until that night, I had a feeling of invincibility. I tested myself in dangerous situations with a sense of fearlessness. I would jump into the water at Lake Powell seeing how long I could stay under before I ran out of air. I'd climb steep hills when we went camping; I'd participate in reckless dares and push my limits to the brink. I had an inner cockiness that came about by hanging out with boys growing up.

I remember playing football with a group of guys, and one tackled me so hard that I lay there with the wind knocked out of me. I popped up pretending it didn't hurt, finished the game, and earned a lot of respect that day. I loved watching the Indianapolis 500; it was bold, brash, challenging, and badass. Someday, I would see the pagoda in person, I told myself. I wanted to push my limits and raise the bar. My uncle Gordon taught me how to play on a pool table, drive a boat, and shoot a shotgun. Forget nail polish or makeup, yet I was still Daddy's girl.

I always felt that I had something to prove, not only to myself but to others as well. My dad had a saying, "Don't tell me about it; just do it."

I think 'the basketball shoe company' stole his saying and made millions when my dad should have made millions.

Those words came back to bite him. At the age of seventeen, I decided to enter the U.S. Air Force. I gave my parents a few weeks' notice about my decision.

They walked around with a look of worry, as they were not ready to let me go. I wanted the challenge, and I would leave as soon as I graduated high school. It was a brash decision for someone who had never left her family before.

Angel Appears

I attended a Catholic church at Lackland Air Force base in San Antonio, Texas. Barely eighteen, I had injured my foot, bad enough for it to swell up. It happened when I was trying to show off, show my comrades an eighteen-year-old could run quicker, faster, and jump higher. It was a preventable injury. Instead of marching in the 101-degree weather in the middle of July, I was assigned to light walking duty for three months. I would accompany female airmen to their doctors' appointments.

I was curious about a large air hangar building and was told that paranormal training took place there. I had asked more than once about UFOs and any classified trainings that were happening. That's where I wanted to be—I wanted to learn how to astral travel. I went to a bar, they didn't check my I.D., and I sat next to an older man in uniform. I asked him about UFOs, and he gave me the *quiet down* gesture. He told me he didn't know about aliens, but he had a buddy who had experience in mental telepathy training. He didn't know how they chose people to work in that unit. I thought it was fascinating; later, I would get my paranormal fix by watching *The X-Files*.

Two months into waiting to be discharged, I was homesick, and the worst part for me was bedtime. At 9:00 p.m. on the dot, the military song "Taps" would play; echoing in the quiet bunker, it brought about a hollow sadness within me every night.

I attended Mass on a Sunday, and there was a buzz in the air, a subtle, positive vibration of energy. I attributed the vibe to all the positive thoughts of the parishioners gathered in a small space. I prayed for the feeling of home, and as though a magic wand had been waved, I felt like I was home again. There was a holiness present which gave me a sense of security and inner peace.

Unfortunately, when I left the chapel, the feeling went away. Within six months I was sent back home to Salt Lake City, Utah, with a renewed sense of faith, though still longing for more proof of divine existence.

After my discharge, I went to Mass every weekend and attended catechism classes. I prayed for God or Creator to show me proof of he/she/it's existence. I wanted concrete proof, visual proof, like seeing a figure in a brilliant ray of light. I wanted to see with my own eyes some sort of miracle.

I attended Catholic Mass for two years, every Sunday praying for physical proof of God, or any kind of proof. Nothing happened.

After figuring my efforts were for nothing, I stopped praying. I started attending Mass at my convenience, which became once a month.

On Memorial weekend, I was coming out of an electronics store on a sunny day and happened to glance up toward the sky for no reason. I didn't feel prompted to; I tilted my head up. What I witnessed took my breath away! Directly above me, I noticed a perfect cloud that was outlined as an angel. I immediately stopped in my tracks, squinted, and blinked my eyes. It was a solid cloud, with a detailed feminine face. She had a small nose, perfect lips, and flowing hair. She was donned with a robe, halo, and beautiful, majestic wings. I stared at her in amazement and was overcome with a forceful feeling of pure, unconditional love. I wanted to cry tears of happiness. It was the most powerful sight and the most exhilarating feeling I had ever sensed! I had never experienced any types of drugs or substances then, but it was an ecstatic natural high.

I said in my mind, "You are beautiful, please don't ever leave me."

Then I glanced about eight feet in front of me and noticed a two-year-old child in a cart. He was reaching up toward the sky with a smile on his face.

I thought, "He sees her too."

As I was watching the young child, I saw his hands drifting from straight up to moving downward. I looked up again, and the angel was trailing off into the distance.

"No, don't leave me! Please stay!" I thought.

I looked around me, and there were other adults, looking straight forward, as though they were wearing blinders. Nobody else noticed this incredible event. Maybe it was only meant for me and the small child. Why didn't anyone else witness or feel her presence? She was there, in plain sight!

Dream Man

I was twenty-seven years old and content with life, employed as a Family Advocate at Head Start. I graduated with a Bachelor of Arts in Family and Human Development from the University of Utah. I spent my weekends with my cousins, aunts, uncles, and parents. I dated here and there, but the dates were always boring, or the compatibility was off. I guess you could say I gave up on ever finding anyone. I declared to my mom and dad, "I think I'm going to stay single forever; marriage isn't for me."

The Universe can be unexpected and comical. That very weekend I told my parents I would become an old maid and live with them forever, the unexpected happened.

I went to my aunt Bobbie and uncle Gordon's house to play cards. As I was sitting at the table, they introduced me to their friends, Roger and Debbie. A nice couple, we played cards for money, and I did well. The lady struck up a conversation with me and said, "I have a son named Daniel, like the Elton John song, I think you would like him."

I was nice and lied, saying I would meet him. In my head, I said, *No. Every mom thinks their son is great.*

I'm sure she is well-meaning, but why can't her son find a date? I laughed to myself and left the party.

Fast forward two weeks later, it's my favorite season, spring, and I am camping with my aunt and uncle. They say, "Debbie and Roger are camping with us. They brought their trailer."

I thought, *Great, I hope she doesn't try and set me up again.*

I walk outside and see a tall guy in a camo outfit, his face covered with a camo mask, looking for something. I walk up to him, and he tells me he lost his arrow. Being the nice person I am, I start looking on the ground with him for the lost arrow.

"Found it!" he announces.

He takes off his camo face mask and confidently introduces himself. "Hello, I'm Daniel." He extends his hand.

The guy is six-foot-three with sparkling green eyes, bright white teeth, and a strong chin. I am taken aback. This guy is handsome and charming, and his mom wants to set us up! Thank you, mama!

"I'm Shell, short for Rachelle," I nervously reply.

We do some small talk, and I head back to the trailer to brush my hair and teeth.

I emerge from the trailer, and he's off riding his four-wheeler. I go back to reading my book. At dinner time, he is at the far end of the picnic table. I grab my plate and glance at him; he's listening to music, bobbing his head.

He notices I am watching him. "It's Fleetwood Mac," he says, as he takes off his headphones. He smiles.

I set my plate in front of him. His face is comforting, he has kind eyes. His lips are full and pink, the best feature of his chiseled face. I'm shy and embarrassed, I can't even eat, and I am speechless. *He's not interested*, I think to myself. I dump my plate and head back into the trailer.

"Where are you going?" he asks.

I sit back down in front of him. He commands the entire conversation and talks about the music he likes; Elton John is a favorite right now. He works as a freight crew manager at night, he knows universal sign language, and he doesn't have a girlfriend! *That could change,* I told myself.

Camping comes to an end the next day; then, as we are leaving, he tells me they are going to Lake Powell in two weeks. My aunt and uncle are going. Would I like to drive down to Powell with him? My heart is pounding, I'm excited, but I tell him I need his phone number and I'll check my schedule; we exchange numbers.

On the day of our trip, I arrive at his house, and his mom is elated to see me. We are pulling two wave runners, and he is driving a Jeep. His parents are driving their motorhome to Lake Powell with us. I look at the house and think to myself, I may be spending a lot of time here. We pull away for our adventure, a bunch of snacks in tow.

There were red flags about him, but I was

blinded. About two hours into the trip, he asks me, "Do you mind if I have a cigarette? I'm not a regular smoker; I occasionally smoke on vacation."

I was honest. "Yes, I do mind. You can't smoke in here. If you want to smoke, you're going to have to pull over and do it." I was adamant.

He pulls over and starts puffing on the cigarette, a major vibe killer for me. He smokes for about eight minutes, then looks at me guiltily.

"Do you need anything? Can I get you a soda or coffee?" he asks.

"I'm good," I say.

We continue our road trip. He puts on a song; it's Pink Floyd's "Wish You Were Here." He is driving and starts singing the song and doing air guitar. He makes me laugh. I love the song, it's my first time hearing it. I ask him to play it again. We keep the song on a loop. We are both singing and playing air guitars and laughing. We do this all the way to Lake Powell. We don't stop for another cigarette break. I am in love with this carefree spirit.

The rest of the week, we hike around the red rocks, ride on the wave runners, and steal secret kisses. On the ride home, we hold hands and sing in the Jeep. Life is good. I have a steady boyfriend now—1998 is the best year of my life.

When I look back at my sex education class in junior high, it was a joke. The kids would snicker. There in front of us was a diagram of a penis and a vagina. We were told about the different parts and their names and shown how to put a condom on a banana. There was not a discussion about personal responsibility, how when a woman says no, it means the man or woman partner stops. Nothing is said to the guys about how birth control is half your responsibility too. To me, sex ed was non-informative for someone that didn't have openness with her parents about sex ed. The message from my conservative parents was don't do it until marriage.

From the first time that Dan and I were intimate, I knew I needed to get on birth control. I called my doctor's office, and my visit was a month away. When I received my prescription, I figured I was good after being on it for a few weeks—well, surprise! I became pregnant. I knew I was about four weeks pregnant when I found out. I loved Dan, but I was unsure of what his reaction would be. I was hoping he would be receptive.

We were driving to his parents' house when I divulged the news.

"I'm pregnant. I took the test twice, and it says I'm pregnant," I confessed.

He slammed on the brakes and pulled over to

the side of the road. He hit the steering wheel with both hands. "You are not having it; I'm not going to be a dad! I'm not ready!" he yelled.

"I think we can make it work," I pleaded.

He then tells me that it's my decision. If I decide to have the baby, he is going to leave me and sign over his rights. He was adamant against having a child. I wasn't ready either. However, I'd always wanted children. I couldn't imagine being a single mom. I wasn't ready financially. I gave in and went to Planned Parenthood the next week for an abortion, which he set up.

It was downtown, and the place looked run down. Daniel was worried but adamant that we needed to do this. I walked into a back room with the nurse, undressed in a gown as if I were visiting a gynecologist. For a moment, I closed my eyes and daydreamed about meeting a man who wanted a baby and a family. He would rescue us, and we would live happily ever after.

Then the doctor came into the room, and I cried on the inside and held myself together on the outside. They inserted a tube into my cervix. I held my breath as I felt a shooting pinch all around my pelvis and stomach area. They told me I would be bleeding for a while, and the pain should subside after a few days.

The physical pain did go away, but the mental pain didn't. I left the clinic and was infertile for many years thereafter. There was no literature given to me. It was as though I had a filling done on my teeth. Yet for me, it was a painfully traumatic experience. I went there in a daze and came out of the clinic with a part of me missing.

I am aware of the polarizing views on abortion. I am thankful that I was able to have a choice about my own life and my own body. To me life is important, but even more important is the gift of free will and choice.

Losing Faith

It is the fall of November 1998 when we notice my dad is tired all the time. A man who never complained was having back pain. He scheduled a doctor visit which was two weeks out. In the meantime, his appetite went away, and we were worried, but not in a panic. The pillar of stability in my life was not his usual self. My mind reasoned it would somehow get better; after all, my dad, Richard Nelson Smith, was a hardworking, strong man with hands of steel. He made time for me in his busy schedule and could never go to bed angry with me. If we had any disagreements, ever, he would come downstairs to my room and apologize.

We would both hug. I'd be in tears, and he would tell me, "Toughen up."

My dad had a mellow temperament, always calm in times of chaos. He was the first to pull over and run to someone's aid if he came upon an accident. Neighbors would knock on our door if they had a plumbing or water leak. He would tease my mom if a neighbor lady came to our door asking for help.

"You better take good care of me, the neighbor ladies won't stop knocking at my door," he would joke.

I laughed because the neighbor lady on the corner was getting a divorce, and she came and told my dad her entire business.

He stood outside and said, "So, he kicked you to the curb?" He smiled.

"No, I kicked him to the curb." She laughed.

Oh my God! Did my dad really say that? Only he could get away with that!

He didn't call me by my name. He would say s*he'awéé*, which in Navajo means "My child."

I know enough Navajo to understand, yet not enough to speak it fluently. Navajo words are filled with emotion, and you get a visual description when the words are spoken. This, to me, makes the language powerful. When he addressed me in Navajo, my interpretation was, "You're my child, who I love." I deeply felt the sentiment behind his words in Navajo. There are tones and pitches for certain words, which allow the language to be expressive and emotional.

Daddy was the person who I knew could get me through anything. To me, he represented true integrity. His work ethic was hard; his honor was important to him. He was selfless, helped others, worked for free, and fixed faucets and air conditioners. You name it, he could fix it.

He couldn't be down for long. Even though

he felt ill, he insisted on going to work. Twelve-hour welding shifts were difficult. His welding was spot on; his work depended upon him, and they gave him a lot of overtime. He would often work late and enter the door limping. My job was to tug his work boots off his feet, which I had skillfully learned to do, pulling from the heel and peeling them off his foot. He would let out a sigh and say thank you.

When my mom told me he was not feeling well, I turned to daily morning prayers. I prayed hard and even brought out my medicine bag Dad had given me. Isn't it strange how many of us suddenly turn to God or Spirit in our most desperate times? We're almost like the people who track you down when they need money.

I was that person with God. My dad was sick, and I believed if I prayed hard and devotedly, he would grant me a favor. After all, I was a deserving good person. I remember the day of Dad's diagnosis clearly. We ended up in the emergency room late one evening in January. My dad had an IV in his arm, and they were taking blood from him. He turned into the one comforting me. I clung to his arm tightly and laid my head on his chest.

He turned to me and said, "It will be ok, *Awéé*, I'll be ok," as he brushed my hair back with his large, leathery hands.

He smiled and said to me, "No matter what happens, you'll always be my little gal."

I remember praying in my mind, begging God, "Please don't let him die."

I bargained with God. I said I would start attending church again, to devote all I have to Him.

Still, after several hours of waiting for his lab work, a CT scan, and draining his stomach of fluid, the young doctor sat us down. My mom, dad, and I were in the hospital hallway, and we held hands.

"We found a lot of cancer in your scan. It's the fatal kind. You have stage IV pancreatic cancer, and it's incurable," the doctor said, with no emotion.

My mom and I cried and held on to my dad. He was in disbelief. We asked how long he had and if he could do treatments. The doctor said only the oncologist would know, but from what he knew, there was nothing that could be done. I was angry with his bluntness and his lack of compassion. I knew I needed to be strong, or at least act strong, for my parents.

Coming to terms with one's fate must be the most difficult challenge a person has to face, no matter what age a person is.

From "How is my family going to go on without me?" to the fearful question of "What will become of me?"

I remember waking up at sunrise the morning after my father's diagnosis, medicine bag in hand, praying for a long time, and begging God to spare my dad. I couldn't comprehend a life without him. I asked God for guidance and a miraculous cure. Later that day, we were sent to an oncologist who eventually confirmed the worst at the hospital.

My dad had adenocarcinoma, the most aggressive type of pancreatic cancer. No treatment would help. We ended up taking him to the University of Utah cancer center, where we were blessed to meet a wonderful oncologist, Doctor Byes. She knew there was no hope, yet she wanted to keep him comfortable and to keep our spirits up. I knew she was heaven-sent—her optimism was contagious, and she spoke directly to my dad as though he were the only one in the room. She gave him fluids and did some chemo treatments, and I am thankful for her presence.

The whole experience of going through my dad being sick hit me hard driving home from work one day. I knew he had incurable cancer, and it became overwhelming. Dizziness settled in, and I had the urge to jump out of the car. I pulled over to the side of the road, my heart pounding, my knuckles clenched, and my palms sweaty. Was I losing it? I stepped out of the car and felt like I had to catch my breath. My face was hot.

Finally, I gave in and cried my eyes out. I had to walk around the parking lot for the next fifteen minutes. I dismissed that moment as a weird incident. It felt like I was going crazy inside, yet I was still alive and functioning. Little did I know, I had experienced my first full-blown panic attack.

Last Moments

The whole month of January 1999 was a blur to me—visits to the cancer treatment center, sitting with my dad, and seeing people of all ages in the chemotherapy chair. My dad insisted on getting treatments; he wanted the extra time, and his doctor obliged.

I took snapshots in my mind and told myself, "Please don't forget his face, his scent, all his quirks, his presence—don't ever forget those qualities."

We sat and watched *Green Acres* during his chemo treatments, and I made sure he had plenty of crackers and liquids. Seeing him smile was a blessing.

Each time I wondered, "How many more times will you let me see his smile, God? Please give us more time."

Even the annoying clearing of his throat no longer bothered me. His slow driving was a blessing, and even him loving the Dallas Cowboys didn't annoy me. He could do no wrong. In that last month, my dad turned into a complete beauty, and I hung on to him until his final breath. In those final months, I transformed from the loving daughter who depended on him so much into him needing me.

At one of the chemo visits, he wore moccasin slippers, and the laces had come undone. He looked at me and asked, "Will you tie them?"

I was upset by this, but I didn't want to make him feel bad. I tied them sloppily and rushed to the restroom in tears. For the longest time, after his death, I regretted not tying them properly.

Now, as I look back, it would have been okay to break down and say, "I love you so much, that's why I cried. I know one day our spirits will be together again."

I remember going home after his treatment, and as we pulled up to the house, Pink Floyd's "Wish You Were Here" played. We listened to the song peacefully together. I turned to my dad after the song was over and said, "Dad, did you like that song?"

In the most real moment we ever had, he turned to me and said, "I don't know what is ahead for me. My thoughts are filled with *what will I become?*" The words came innocently—like a child. "I heard some of the song," he said.

I turned the radio down and said the only thing I could think of: "I love you, Dad," and "Somehow I know you're going to be ok."

We embraced and cried. We'd been staying strong for each other. It was a relief to let go for a minute. I got a smile out of him after we hugged, and it was beautiful.

In my mind, I believe when I hear the song "Wish You Were Here," it's my dad saying, "I'm still here, and yes, without anything to worry about, I like the song."

My father's first grandbaby, Cherelle Smith, was about to be born—my sister-in-law, Amy, was due any day with a baby girl. From the day my dad heard he would be a grandpa, he was so excited for her arrival.

Even in his sickened state, by March he was asking every day, "Is the baby here yet?"

I remember the day my niece was born: Sunday, March 21, 1999. She entered the world in the morning, and given our unusual circumstances, that night she was released to visit her grandfather Richard. That whole period is a saddened fog to me, but I remember the moment she was brought in to visit with my dad. He had become bedridden the day before, a sudden turn for the worse. The family had come to visit from New Mexico and Arizona; they were all gathered at his bedside. His sisters and various cousins were there.

My sister-in-law brought the newborn into my dad's room. She brought her into a sorrow-filled room. For the first time, my dad's face lit up with a beaming smile. It was as though God gave him one last moment of heaven on Earth. He suddenly had strength. He lifted his arms and reached for her; he was excited and happy. The demeanor of the room lightened, and we had smiles on our faces. He held her in his arms for a couple of minutes. To me, it was an eternity. He kissed her on the forehead, and there wasn't a dry eye in the room as we all burst into tears of joy.

But as soon as he handed her back, his body slumped over, and his state turned even worse; he had accomplished his goal of seeing his granddaughter, and now it was his time to transition. I stayed awake, holding my dad's hand until midnight. He seemed uncomfortable, with sweat on his forehead, heart racing, and in utter agony. I prayed for God not to let him suffer, and I went to bed with feelings of guilt because I could not bear watching him die.

I woke up and went straight to my dad's room. I was told he didn't sleep at all and refused to take pain pills. As I touched his hand and put my cheeks against his, my mom took his other hand, and we both said we loved him. He took a last breath and then seemed to turn cold. From that moment on, a hollow emptiness entered. The most important part of me, my sense of security, was whisked away. I wanted to feel his spirit leave, but that didn't happen, which disappointed me.

At that moment, I was fiercely angry at God. Why did He take such a good man? If you exist, God, why didn't you let me feel his spirit leave? Why did he have to suffer? I was in a blinding rage later that night.

I yelled, "I hate you because you let my daddy die!"

I felt like God had abandoned me or maybe He/She/It didn't exist?

I tossed my medicine bag and my cross into a junk drawer. I didn't care about God or faith, and I said it aloud. "If you exist, I don't believe in you anymore, you're not powerful!"

At that moment, I heard a group of crows squawking outside on top of the garage. I ran outside and grabbed a couple of rocks. I missed, but I threw them as hard as I could and yelled, "GO AWAY ASSHOLES! I hate you!"

Deep inside, there was rage brewing, yet my outward demeanor was that of being silent and withdrawn. I disengaged from the world.

Losing my father didn't make sense to me. It was hard for me to understand, hard to justify. Why was he taken away? It felt like I was being punished. All my life, I followed all the rules: I didn't steal, lie, or cheat. I said my prayers. I remember it being a rainy day, and I pulled over and gave an older lady my umbrella. I kept score in my head of all my good deeds. I figured this existence was like a board game; if I was righteous, goodness would be bestowed upon me, and I could win the game of life. How could I not? Funny, I had the feeling I was being watched, like Jim Carrey in *The Truman Show*.

Somebody had to be keeping score. Losing my dad was surreal, heartbreaking, and one big blur.

I was picking out a burial outfit for my dad at JCPenney's. I walked around thinking, "My dad never will walk me down the aisle. I can't believe this; what happened? Did we not go to the right doctor? Was he being punished? Could I have done something to make the outcome different?"

We had Mass and a eulogy at the Catholic church in Page, Arizona. The church was packed. I looked around and knew he was well-respected, that people looked up to him, that he was a man who would be greatly missed. As Mass ended, I said goodbye to my dad. I touched his head and kissed him. I walked out of the church and looked at the sky. The dark clouds parted as if on cue, and within seconds, majestic rays from the sun were beaming upon me.

A voice in my head said, "This is your sign."

Joy filled my heart at that moment. "I love you, Creator, I'm sorry," I said aloud.

I made peace with God that day and made it a goal to reconnect with my spiritual side. I thought this was my darkest moment of despair and tragedy. However, it was only the beginning. I couldn't imagine my life getting any worse. When your world is crashing down, when the stars are no longer aligned, that's when the real spiritual journey begins. Author Joseph Campbell called it "The Dark Night of the Soul." All of us go through it.

Like a Snowflake

You displayed your beauty, floating effortlessly on a warm moon winter night.

Like a snowflake falling, you were shiny; you were glistening, you were bright.

We will always remember your words, your will, your pride.

In quiet moments, when all is still, in you I still confide.

Your touch is within everything, even if I can't hear your voice in a phone call.

I will wait for you; for your presence is within the first snowfall.

Baby Bliss

I married my husband Daniel in July 2000, a year after losing my father. After the storm of losing my dad, there was a sense of peace shortly thereafter.

We bought a house that was built in the 1980s, with a well-maintained yard, in a religious Latter-Day Saint neighborhood. Living in Utah was my life; I enjoyed the mountains, the skiing, and the fry sauce. Fry sauce, family home evenings, and a church on every corner is a Utah thing. Across the street was a police patrol car that belonged to my neighbor; it gave me an extra sense of safety. We lived in a neighborhood where you could leave your door unlocked and everyone looked out for one another. The neighbors behind us grew fresh corn, and they brought us fresh eggs from their chickens daily. It was my utopia, how I pictured every neighborhood should function. My husband had a thriving business with two helpers, and we had more material wealth than my middle-class parents had provided me. The lawn was manicured weekly, and to top it off, I had a great job at a place where I made a difference. I was invited to be a guest speaker at a ritzy hotel in Park City. The topic was personalities in the workplace. I had always dreamed of public speaking. Life seemed perfect.

I took a deep breath and could smell the soothing aroma of a fresh turkey baking. After three years of trying to get pregnant, it finally happened! Even without an ultrasound, I could sense it was a boy. My loving husband, Daniel, knew turkey was my primary pregnancy craving. He painted and put trim in the baby room, assembled the crib, and painted the walls a buttercream yellow. Love and comfort surrounded our home.

I felt in flow and said, "Thank You," out loud.

A defining moment for me happened when I entered the shower. The sweet smell of fresh lavender tingled my nasal passages as it funneled through the open window of the shower. I heard the high-pitched sound of crickets chirping as the sun set. I peeked out my steamy window and saw a crow perched on the white picket fence. It cawed at me as if to say, "Yes, you are blessed."

I thought that maybe one day I might need to hold on to this moment to keep my sense of sanity. I was unaware that my life could take a complete turnaround in a mere blink of an eye. Being in a state of grace was comforting; however, it also kept me shielded away. It allowed me to focus on my family and my neighborhood community. Yet at the same time, I was naïve about drug addiction and poverty.

Though I was a social worker with empathy, I didn't know how someone could get themselves in such a bind where they couldn't afford shoes for their child or how they couldn't take their child to the doctor when they were sick or feed them breakfast in the morning. I had sympathy, but a part of me was judgmental. Fortunately, I had my backups, my safety nets, and a plan for emergencies. There was plenty of cash on hand, credit cards, a safety deposit box, a money market fund, retirement, savings bonds, and life insurance. An extended warranty on everything I bought; it all made sense to me, and I could not see living life any other way.

Darkness of Addiction

Pull down that hood, nobody's watching, nobody hears.

This one time, to break the monotony, to take away the fears.

Nobody can see, it's my secret, it's forbidden I know.

I can cheat, I can steal, I can lie, for me the stakes are low.

Keep it hidden, keep it out of sight, oh no, I'm losing the fight.

I keep doing it, to feel normal, I know this isn't right.

My spirit is breaking, my body can't take it anymore.

Yet in my riddled mind, all I can think of is

the next score.

Will I conquer my inner demons? Take control of my fate?

Or will I give in and try to enter heaven's gate?

Addiction

My husband had knee surgery a month before our wedding and began taking prescription painkillers. He admitted to chasing after pills even after they were no longer prescribed to him. His moods without the pills varied from withdrawn to angry; he was addicted. I made an inner decision to cure him, which became my internal battle. I wanted my son to have a dad, and I wanted the man I'd first met to come back.

There were warning signs early on in our relationship—I'd overlooked them. Small lies about money, lies about what substances he had used in the past. Then, the pain pill addiction turned everything into a tidal wave of deception. He was lying, stealing, and going against every value I stood for. What did I do? I looked the other way; I was more worried about losing the house, a foundation for our son. I was in survival mode.

I had my son, a twelve-month-old baby, in the car. It was midnight. Using an ATM, I checked out $600.00, so I could bail my son's father out of jail. By the time his dad was processed out, it was 2:00 a.m., and I had to work the next day.

At the lowest of many lows, it was the middle of July, and my two-year-old son was sitting in the heat. It was smoldering hot, and of course, my husband had spent our money on drugs. Our power was shut off. I had to lay outside on a mattress with my baby because there was no A/C. I felt like the worst mother in the world. Every day I'd wake up, and instead of welcoming the new day, I'd dread it, wondering what the next calamity would be.

One day I arrived home from work to find my husband gone. Where was he? Suddenly, there's a loud banging at the front door. I open it to find the Park City SWAT team with their guns pointed at me. I was already numb. I gazed into the gun barrels. They put the guns down when they saw I had a child in my arms. It seemed like a bad dream. I told myself, "Ok, it can't get any worse than this," but to my dismay, it did. My son was only half asleep in my arms. They asked if Dan was home. I told the officer I had not seen him. They searched the house, overturning things. The bathroom door was shut; they kicked it in. The man looked at me like I could potentially be hiding him and could be an addict myself!

I said, "I have a job, a baby, and to be honest, is it really necessary to kick in the door?"

His demeanor changed, and he told me, "Your husband was supposed to be in court for a drug charge; he has an outstanding warrant. You need to notify us when you see him."

I told him, "I was just here for a change of clothes, and we'll be sleeping at my mom's, where he is not welcome."

The officers left, and again I was left questioning my devotion to this man. I went to my mom's house and hid the truth from her. I hid the truth from everyone. I went to work. I did not mention anything.

My husband eventually called me and told me a story. He said he did not have drugs on him; they were a legal prescription, and the pills were just not in the bottle. I believed him. I did not call the police to inform them he was sleeping at the house from midnight to 5:00 a.m. and took off mostly to chase pills all day. He justified his behavior, and I justified that I needed him because he was the father of my child.

The house where we lived did not like the presence of my husband. When I was alone with my son at the house, all was peaceful and well. As soon as he came home, cupboards would slam. On two occasions, he sat by the fireplace, and the window in the fireplace shattered from the inside out, right next to where he was sitting!

He justified it each time, "It must be a small bird." My instincts told me it was something greater.

Day by day, I was desensitized to the chaos that my husband was creating. One day he came home with a pile of groceries. We had been hurting for money, and it was a welcome sight. Then he said, "They are stolen." Every inch of my being was against this act, yet in desperation, I hastily put the groceries away. He assured me that this was only temporary.

I was now in the ranks with all the single moms that I helped daily. Finally, I knew how one could not maintain the necessities with an addict living in the house. It drains you physically, mentally, and financially. I was now standing in line at the grocery store, trying to figure out how to make dinner with $5.00. It was enough to make spaghetti without meat and buy a two-liter soda to lessen the feelings of hunger. I was too proud to show up at Mom's house, too ashamed to tell anyone that I couldn't feed my family. I realized that being poor cost me more than having money.

When I had money, I bought all the extended warranties; everything that became broken was fixed for free. Being poor, I bought the cheapest product, which broke after a couple of months; then the cycle of buying the cheapest products continued.

I was going through the motions of life and didn't know who I was. It was as though I was in a boat in the middle of the ocean with no oars, miserably floating, waiting for the rescue boat. Except, there was no rescue boat coming. There never is.

When I was younger, I molded myself to be what my parents wanted me to be, which was respectful, obedient, and unselfish. Then when I married, I molded myself to be what my husband wanted me to be, which was someone who was always in agreement with him.

The fact my parents expected subservience from me did not serve me well when I needed to stand up for myself. When we moved into our house, I started emulating the neighbors around us. I wanted to keep up with the Joneses, have a nice house, nice lawn, and the weekend barbecues. I liked those things, but small talk and frivolous conversations were not me. When it was time for me to leave this environment that I had grown accustomed to, I found myself grasping on to it for dear life, holding on to a fake existence that no longer belonged to me.

Working full time, I had to concentrate on my job along with a baby. My husband would start a new job, then he would be fired.

He didn't tell me his truth: "I'm a drug addict, and I was pulled over for possession along with being high." His excuse would be, "I'm in jail because of a broken windshield and a mud flap violation. I had one beer and failed their test."

I would come home from work to find him passed out and unresponsive on the bed, knowing he had a warrant. When he would go to jail, I'd bail him out so he could get to his new job and avoid being fired.

I now understood the saying, "You don't know what people are really going through."

When I arrived at work, my mind would be so occupied with thoughts ranging from worrying about my son getting a cold to fearing that my husband might have a warrant or be dead soon. I feared what would become of my son without his dad. I thought that I needed to fight harder to be a better wife, then he would change.

I would walk into work and do my job, but there was a lingering cloud hovering over my head. The once outgoing, happy-go-lucky girl was now withdrawn. It was becoming hard to get through my days at work. What I used to do with ease became difficult. My original supervisor was caring and helpful and could read me like a book. She brought comfort and encouragement, allowing me to maintain an average work performance as I was going through my catastrophic storm. I would go to work, not remembering which route I had taken to get there. I'd put on my game face, pretending all was okay when deep inside I was unraveling.

It was Christmas, and my husband was arrested for stealing, drug possession, and a suspended license. I decided to skip town.

By then I had an eight-year-old son and was depressed about my situation. I left to see my family in Page, Arizona. I thought about leaving my husband and starting a new life somewhere else. My body was in flight or fight mode all the time; everything startled me.

As I sat with my grandmother and my aunties, a sense of peace and comfort came back to my spirit. My aunt Lori had brought about five different flavors of ice cream. All of us women—four aunts, four girl cousins, and my grandmother—sat around a table eating ice cream and laughing until we cried. Gathering with family, laughing, sharing, and acknowledging each other—these moments were special.

Going back to my second home was nice, and the fact that he was in jail was a relief. I knew he wasn't abusing drugs there, and he was safe. I was able to focus on myself and what my next small goals would be, like finding a new place to live.

I always had hope around this time because he was ordered to go to rehab, and I thought, "Maybe he will beat his addiction this time."

I clung on with high hopes. And yes, things were good after he came home from rehab until the unthinkable happened.

Losing Me

Things went well after my husband's stint in rehab. When things went well, everything was amazing. My husband was a charming, funny, adventurous being. A man who made a damn good chicken fettuccine alfredo and barbecue ribs like no other. He was a doting dad, he would pull my son in the wagon, visit with the neighbors, fix my car, and so much more. I was finally starting to feel good and get back into my routine again.

He was three months sober; life was good. When sober, he put his efforts into others. He would buy an extra-large bag of popsicles, walk to the park, and engage with my son and the other children there. I would sit back and watch him help a little girl swing or he would help my son climb on the monkey bars. I wondered in my head, "My love, if you are happy at this moment, why do you need substances? Are we not enough for you?"

Then thoughts of other addicted family members would pop into my head. My sweetest uncle, Junior, battled addiction. He wasn't afraid to say, "Niece, I love you." He was the first person to give the coat off his back to someone. Unfortunately, even his kind heart could not save him from addiction.

One Friday night my husband didn't come home. His phone was going straight to voicemail—something was off. I took my son to my mom's house and spent the night looking for him until 4:00 a.m. the next morning. Worried and exhausted, I fell asleep and woke up at 7:00 a.m. in the morning. I found a piece of paper with the address of Abanadi Road in his pant pockets. I looked up the address and found a street by the same name which belonged to a house across town. I found the street tucked against the serene mountainside. His truck was in front of a large mansion with a long driveway.

My mind told me he could be dead. I nervously knocked on the front door, but nobody answered. I went to the back of the house and opened the sliding glass door and walked into the empty house. There was no sign of him upstairs or in all the rooms downstairs. I searched outside in the back of the property and found nothing. Then I spotted a door leading to the garage. I opened the door, and on the ground was the man I loved, face down. My head went into a spin, my heart was racing. I ran to him and dropped to my knees.

I said aloud, "Please God, don't take my

son's dad, he needs a father, please!"

I immediately wanted to call an ambulance, but three days prior, I found out he had a warrant again. He told me, "If I have to go to jail again, I will just go ahead and kill myself."

His face was ashen. I touched his hands; they were still warm! I checked his pulse, and he had one. I listened for his breath. He was still breathing! I shook his arm and called out his name. His eyes were rolling all about, but he was still alive! I ran inside and grabbed a glass of water, a washcloth, and pillows. I put a washcloth on his head and started to check his pockets and found two pill bottles. One was labeled as OxyContin, the other was labeled Xanax. They were both half full. I put them in my pocket. I propped him up with pillows and tried to talk to him. He was out of it, in a drunken stupor. I reasoned he needed to rest. Hopefully, he could come to his senses. His breathing seemed to be okay.

I wanted to discard the root of evil, the pills. He needed food and water, so I left him lying on his side.

As I drove down a steep hill, I spotted a large garbage can. I threw the fucking pills away at the bottom of the street. I then drove to a burger drive-through. At the window my heart raced, my mouth was dry, and my head was foggy. My body shivered as though I was cold. I wondered if I was losing my mind? There was a car in front of me and one behind me; I felt trapped. Something inside my head told me to visualize my most peaceful moment. I was back in the shower again. I felt the shower droplets and smelled the flowers. The visualization calmed me enough to get to the drive-through window. I was still disoriented but managed to order food and drinks. I dismissed the incident and drove back to the house to find him sitting on the ground.

He sat there in a daze and asked me, "What

happened?"

I said, "You took too many pills and almost died."

I gave him a sack of food and water. He lightly sipped on the water. Then he frantically began to check his pockets. He walked to his truck and started tearing it apart. He was manically looking for the pills I had thrown away. I felt hopeless—my efforts were for nothing. I was up all night and had found him looking dead, and now all he cared about were two bottles of pills. Wasn't he happy to be alive?

"Did you see any bottles?" he asked. I lied. "No."

"If you took them, that's part of our house payment. I was selling them for $20 apiece, I need to find them."

I looked him straight in the eyes. "I don't know where they are," I said in a cold voice.

I left the property and came back to check on

him six hours later. He was still frantically looking everywhere for the pill bottles. This was serious. This was dire. The man I loved was completely consumed by pills. On his current path, he was headed for death.

It was a clear message for me to leave, yet where would I go? I had my mom, relatives, and friends who would gladly take us in. Yet, I was too proud and ashamed to admit I was in a deep mess. I didn't want to rely on anyone but myself. Leaving also meant he would show up at their house, trying to get us back. We were codependent on each other; I allowed him to come back to me every time he was caught with drugs. He worked, made the house payment, and he was a good enough dad. Still, both of our actions were perpetuating an unhealthy cycle.

I had glimpses of hope. I found myself praying every day in the church chapel. I would beg and plead with God to change him. I found myself latching on to people who seemed to be able to help me or who seemed to have it together. I wanted to figure out their secret of being normal. How did they have such an amazing life, yet mine was in shambles?

I went to work in a daze. I did the minimum at work when I used to do extra. At my worst point physically and mentally, I was living on autopilot, going through the motions of existence. I was a good person, trying to do all the right things, but I wasn't present in the moment. I did what I thought I needed to do. Be a mom, wife, and good employee; showing a false front that everything was fine. Inside, my confidence was low, and I didn't trust myself. I doubted my decisions, I questioned my abilities, and I looked to others for the answers to my life.

I imagined if I broke down crying and told someone what was going on in my life, I would only bother them. I thought I'd be perceived as weak and less than—as if I was not trying hard enough.

If anyone at work said, "How are you, Shell?" I would reply with a smile, "Fine."

I wasn't fine, and I didn't know whether my husband was out getting high or if I could pay the bills!

Being the partner to an addict was draining—every extra dollar was hoarded by him, and every cent was spent on drugs, that all-consuming, mind-altering facade. It was a battle for me to become better than the drugs. I felt I could fix my husband by being more logical, more loving, and more on top of it. Those of you who have ever known or lived with a drug addict know that there is nothing you can say or do to compete with an addict's drugs. I was no match. It wasn't my fault.

My thoughts dwelled on, "If I can get him into the right rehab. If I can show him how important he is and how much his son needs him."

His drug use was outside of my control, yet it became my mission to keep him sober. Each time, I ran smack into a brick wall, and each relapse put a scar on my soul. I blamed myself each time. Should I have kept the money from him? Should I have checked his pockets? The burden of his addiction consumed my entire thoughts.

My nine-year-old son once said something so enlightening that it blew me away. He asked his dad point blank, in front of his therapist, Allison, "Dad, I need to know why you take drugs."

His dad answered, "Because I'm in pain."

My son said, "Did you know that when people feel pain, it means they are alive? It's you being alive, Dad."

What a brilliant comment, and now when I have the occasional ache or pain, I tell myself, "Remember you're alive."

How bad was my mental health? I was now waking up and looking forward to bedtime, the only time I could turn off my brain and not think about the big mess I was in—a physical, emotional, spiritual, and financial mess.

Now my panic attacks were happening whenever I would walk out the door, but I kept pushing myself.

I was working full time, and my co-workers loved going out to eat. I loved it too. We would eat, laugh, and banter back and forth.

But what once seemed natural was now a hard task. My heart would start beating rapidly, my mouth would dry up, and I had difficulty swallowing. I would wring my hands, and they would be sweaty and cold. I would try to show up for an event, and I would stay for as long as I could, but after ten minutes, I would make up an excuse and leave. I didn't know it at the time, but I was training my brain to avoid social situations. In my mind, I made up a story, "You're introverted, you prefer to be alone, this is temporary."

I woke up one day in the deepest depths of depression. I went outside, trying to pinpoint where my angst was coming from. I was having trouble just taking a full breath of air in, then panic would sweep over me.

I thought, "What if this is my new existence? What if I wake up like this every day? Am I broken?"

I remember laying down at night and being thankful for nighttime because I wanted to escape from reality. Each morning I woke up, I had hopes that my life would be different. I wanted to wake up without fear, without the feeling of doom and despair. Yet, each day I was met with the same unpleasant feelings.

As soon as my eyes opened, I knew I was in for a day of struggle. I would lay there, get up, and would walk to the corner. I had to keep reminding myself to breathe; damn, even breathing was no longer natural! I was somehow inadvertently holding my breath and taking shallow breaths. I was forgetting how to do something that was supposed to be innate.

My life as I knew it was now over. It seemed as if nothing could make me feel better, nothing could fix me from the depths of darkness. My whole act for the entire day was trying to appear normal to everyone that I encountered. It felt as though I had come out of alignment with my body. I wanted to crawl out of my skin and jump into a hole.

As the days went on, I turned to prayer. I did visualization, looked for cures in books, watched videos, and tried to maintain optimism. Taking my life did come to my mind briefly when I was having a full-blown panic attack.

One of my worst days ever was when I looked at the big, beautiful blue sky and saw the sun brilliantly shining. There was so much magnificence on display, yet inside, I was empty, with a hollowness in the pit of my stomach. If I had to see my therapist or my doctor to get my prescription, it would consume my thoughts the entire night before. I would have my water bottle in hand, and someone would drive me to my appointment.

By the end of the day, I was exhausted with daily panic attacks. I would lie my head down on the pillow, and I'd be out, only to wake up feeling like I couldn't get out of bed. I would take gulps of air, and my head would be cloudy. I didn't have the energy to cry. I was a walking void, my life was that of an ant, wandering from point A to point B.

On one particularly bad day, I found myself in the emergency room with stomach spasms and an inability to catch my breath. The doctor asked me if I took drugs or drank energy drinks. I said no.

He told me, "Your heart rate is extremely high, we'll keep you here until it comes down. Your EKG and other tests are normal, but we will send you to a heart specialist. From what I can tell, it is anxiety. Look at it this way, you're getting a free workout. Do your parents have a history of mental illness?"

"Not my adoptive parents," I answered.

"How about your biological parents?" he asked.

"I don't know them." I said.

"That's unfortunate." The words come matter-of-fact from him.

I'm already a mess, and he told me that? I left the office more depressed than when I first went in. In my state of mind, I wondered if he felt sorry for me, or if he only needed my information to help him make a diagnosis.

I thought of my biological parents. I remembered the report I read, which I came across by accident in my adoptive parents' file cabinet. It said that my biological mother was married and had five other children. My biological father was in the military and was nineteen years old at the time of my birth. I looked at the information and figured I was an affair, an unplanned pregnancy. I felt that I belonged with my adoptive family. I never longed for my biological parents. To me, it was how my cards fell. However, I did wonder about my biological siblings. Did we look alike? Did they know about me? Did we have similar interests?

When I went to a heart specialist, the doctor determined that I had anxiety and agoraphobia. I was physically healthy but a mental mess. When I read his report that I was diagnosed with agoraphobia and anxiety, I was livid. It felt like I was being judged and labeled, and the diagnosis left me feeling shameful. Was I missing something by not knowing my biological parents? I didn't miss them, or at least I didn't believe so.

The doctor told me my heart scan was fine and that I'd passed the stress test. He told me because of all the stress on my body, I was developing a panic reaction and that I needed medication to counteract the reaction. My husband already was a mess on medication, so I didn't want to be medicated! Still, I was desperate. He prescribed me Buspar and a limited amount of Xanax for traveling. It took me a good month to get used to the medication, but I told myself that it was only temporary.

I was immediately drawn to Xanax; I took it and felt invincible for the first time. It took away my panic and gave me confidence. Deep down, I knew that it could become a habit, and it wasn't the way I wanted to live. When I took it, I was well again, a bit too well. I ventured out and flirted; it gave me a strong sense of fake confidence. I knew it could easily destroy me, and I could very well become an addict like my husband.

I went to various therapists, and during these sessions, I realized I had to make a difficult choice. I needed to leave my husband. Being that he was the father of my son, I felt guilt. I didn't want my son to grow up without a father, even if he was an addict. However, I knew the safety of my child came first. Drugs in the house were not something I wanted him to be around. I had to time my exit from my house, like a top-secret operation so he wouldn't freak out on me. I knew I had to leave when he wasn't there and that I had to get my family involved. We all came with about three vehicles and gutted the place in three hours. It was a difficult day, and when he did find out, he made threats to harm himself and accusations that I didn't try hard enough.

I loved this man. I loved him off the pills and

despised him on them.

Dream Premonition

From a young age my dreams had always been elaborate and vivid; sometimes prophetic. Spirit communicated with me in a dream state more often when I would ask for guidance. I had one particularly vivid dream, as I was going through the turmoil of agoraphobia and anxiety. I was in a room with people who were all lying on the floor. I looked around me, some people just lay there, and others were trying to sit up, but couldn't. It reminded me of a hurt ant, writhing in pain.

I panicked and thought, "I can't lay here! I'm going to die here!"

It took all my might to try and stand up. I took two steps and fell. I couldn't walk, so I started slowly crawling to the door. After what seemed like hours, I finally reached the door. I grabbed the doorknob and lifted myself, thrust the door open, and fell out on the other side.

I was inside what seemed like a mall or an airport with high white ceilings. I needed help walking; I opened a closet door and found a mask and a cane. I grasped the cane and put the mask on. I started limping around the gigantic white building, looking for an exit. I was embarrassed about my limp; I wanted to walk in a normal manner. Then I spotted a gigantic, arching, white-framed window.

There was an elevator which I took toward the exit. I looked up and saw that the light of day was shimmering through the glass. When I descended to the bottom, I saw the exit, took off my mask, and triumphantly threw it up in the air.

"I am free," came to mind. My dream abruptly ended.

Car Accident

On October 21, 2011, I was existing, going through the motions of life. The Sunday before, I watched an IndyCar race at Las Vegas Motor Speedway. In that race, a big accident happened where a race car driver, Dan Wheldon, passed away. It weighed heavily on my mind. I thought this guy had it all, and then, *poof*, he was suddenly gone.

It seemed like just another day; I wasn't expecting anything out of the ordinary. I was now two months into taking a low dose of Xanax every morning. I would have to see my doctor soon since I had consumed the last pill earlier that morning. It also worried me that I felt the urge to take more and I would be asking for a higher dose.

I went through a day's work, then headed home. I wanted a fountain Coke, so I asked my niece Serena and my son Dante if they wanted to go to the gas station around the corner with me. They both said no, so I got in my car and drove to the gas station. It was dusk.

I bought my drink and traveled home a different way than how I'd come. I headed west and noticed there was construction. It was getting dark, and I remembered Dan Wheldon. I had the thought, "I wonder if he felt pain in his last moments?" I don't know why the thought popped into my head.

Abruptly, I crashed. The airbags of my car smacked into my face. My head felt like it was pounded by a sledgehammer. I blacked out for what I thought was a few seconds. My whole face hurt, and I could smell blood. I was breathing in the smoke from the airbag;

it burned my lungs and eyes.

I suddenly thought, "My son! My niece!" I was in pain all over but managed to undo my seat belt and look back toward the empty seats. Thank God they weren't there. I tried to take a deep breath, but no air would come in. I panicked, "I can't breathe!"

Something inside my head told me to calm down, so I calmed myself down and air came through. I was breathing lightly; I didn't want a closed airway again. I jarred open the car door and realized I'd driven into a three-foot hole the size of two car lengths. I called 911, and an ambulance was sent. I hung up with the dispatcher and called my mom and aunt.

In a daze, I said a Hail Mary prayer. I sat on the edge of the curb with a high-pitched ringing in my ears. I looked at the hole which the workers forgot to put the grate grill over. My head was pounding, my thoughts were jumbled. I felt as though I was hit in the head with a baseball bat. I sat for a while with my head down, and people saw my car. They saw me in bad shape, but nobody stopped to check on me.

Finally, after what seemed like hours, but was probably around ten minutes, the ambulance and a policeman came to the scene. Pulling up to me, the police officer almost ended up in the hole with me because it was dark now. The paramedics said I had whiplash, but they weren't sure if I had a head injury. They gave me the choice to either go to the hospital or to go home and wait to see if I felt better.

To tell the truth, I should have gone with them, but I was afraid of getting a panic attack. I wanted the comfort of my home. My mom and aunt pulled up to the scene to take me home. My house was right around the corner. The paramedics asked me questions, but I was unresponsive; I couldn't even understand some of their questions. Still, they let me go home with my mom and aunt.

We arrived home, and I went to the couch. I wanted darkness. My mom and aunt went to retrieve my things from the towing facility. They left me with my niece. I stayed on the couch staring ahead into the darkness. My head was throbbing, but I just stared ahead in a daze. I told my mom and aunt I was okay.

I had no idea if I really was. I stared into nothingness for what seemed like minutes, but I was told later that hours had passed. I was completely out of it; I fell asleep and woke up with my head throbbing. I called for help, to no avail. I heard earth-shattering snores from my family; they were all in a deep sleep. Alone, I stood up and was off balance; my head was throbbing. I was confined to the couch. I forced myself to close my eyes, and eventually I fell into a slumber.

I went to the hospital the next day to find that

I had a moderate concussion with a brain bleed that had stopped at the base of my neck. I was prescribed amitriptyline, and it knocked me out, so I tossed it in the garbage. I was told to see a neurologist; the appointment was set two weeks away.

I felt like I was in a bubble. My memory was horrible; simple things had become difficult. My mom set a bowl of cereal in front of me, but I didn't know where the spoons were. I drank the cereal and milk from the bowl. When I finished, I remembered they were in a drawer. I opened the drawer, and they were there. I forgot that I even had to use the bathroom or eat—all the simple things we take for granted.

My body was off. I couldn't navigate my way in the darkness, so I had to sleep with a nightlight. Each night, it felt like ants were crawling across my forehead. At the same time, I had the worst migraine of my life. I got up, took 800 milligrams of ibuprofen, and just lay there. I lay for hours with no relief and finally pleaded, "God, Jesus, please, if you are with me, please take away my pain or just let me fall asleep."

I pictured what Jesus would look like; I visualized myself asking for his help and Him healing me. I drifted to sleep.

I woke up the next day feeling rested, and the crawling ant feeling in my head was gone. I wondered if my prayers were heard?

Agoraphobia

Agoraphobia is defined as an extreme or irrational fear of crowded spaces or enclosed public places. I went laser tagging a year after my car accident. My balance and short-term memory were bad, but I told myself I needed to get out of the house. I found out that what used to be a fun adrenaline rush had turned into a claustrophobic nightmare for me.

The entire lights went off, the doors closed shut, and everything was glowing. I remember having the thought, "I'm trapped."

Then my search for the exit began. While

people were laughing as dizzying lights whisked all over, I searched. After five minutes, I finally found the exit sign in bold lights. I gave my laser gun to a random kid and headed toward the restroom.

My heart was beating quickly as I splashed my face with water. I wondered, what was happening to me? I calmed myself down, and my friends came out. I told them I had to use the restroom.

We walked outside, and my mind told me, "You're safe."

Physically, I was back to myself again. I had a normal heartbeat, there was no sweating, and I was okay. Still, I told myself, you're not going there again. There was safety in running to my car and heading home.

This act of running back home calmed my irrational fears. But from that point on, an exit sign would become the new metaphor for my life. I would hide from everything in life. I would lie to people to get out of anxiety-inducing situations. I could not admit that I was scared. I craved safety and reassurance. I was fearful, I was weak.

I eventually could not return to work and lost my job. I was pushed over the edge mentally and physically. Frequently off balance and in a fog for a few years, I couldn't drive or leave the house for three years. This is when the extreme agoraphobic tendencies and debilitating panic kicked in. I would walk to the corner, and if I walked around the corner, my heart would pound, and my hands would become sweaty. Forget driving, I had someone transport my son to and from school daily.

I would walk around the corner, and like a switch, my face would turn red. My heart would beat fast, and my throat would tighten up. It scared me when I couldn't swallow. I would always carry a bottle of water with me so my mouth wouldn't be dry.

By the time I was done with my short walk, my hands would be trembling, and I would feel lightheaded. I eventually quit attempting to leave the house, and I stayed inside my perceived comfort zone. I made inner boundaries inside my head; my house and yard were my havens. Anywhere else was dangerous. As soon as I walked outside of my imaginary boundaries, it was as though a loaded gun was put to my head. Suddenly, my safety and security were gone, replaced with fear, despair, and a dreaded feeling of impending doom.

My family knew I wasn't myself, but I assured them I was okay even though I wasn't. I didn't want to admit what a mess I was, and I didn't want to be a burden to them. I told them I couldn't go anywhere because I had a stomachache or that my car wasn't working. I paid people to do my grocery shopping. I knew that I had a big problem! I wanted to change but had no clue how. My mom called my grandmother Sue

FINDING MY SACRED

and my aunt Lori, who drove seven hours to be by my side and give their support to me.

Grandma Sue

"Sorrow shared is sorrow lessened."
– *"The Sun Does Shine,"* by Anthony Ray Hinton

My grandmother is my everything. She is my past, my present, and my future. I look into her eyes, and I see depth, love, and my culture. From early on, I aspired to be resilient like my grandmother, Sue Martin Tsosie, who discovered Antelope Canyon in Page, Arizona, at the age of twelve. Her demeanor was strong, and her love for us was immense.

One day, during a car ride home, I asked my grandmother (my mom translated), "What is a memory that sticks out with you the most?"

She told me her tragic story, one no mother should have to tell, with powerful conviction. It's a day embedded in my mind, which still resonates with me now. I cannot help but think that her human existence was so much more troublesome than that of the average person.

She then began her haunting true story. She was a young mother with small children at home. Her husband, my grandfather Shank Tsosie, was busy working on the railroads at least a half day's ride from where they resided. They lived in a small stone house on the vast Arizona reservation. Navajos were nomadic and would travel between their summer and winter homes. Her responsibility was to cook, be a caregiver, and tend to the sheep, horses, and cattle.

One day, it was becoming late, and her eleven- and twelve-year-old daughters had not yet returned from herding the sheep. She was very worried; soon it would be dark, and she would not be able to look for them. A feeling of dread overcame this young mother who was forced to make a split-second decision. She couldn't leave her daughters to the elements of the land. All the w*hat-ifs* went through her head including, "What if a snake bit one of them?" "What if they were hurt? Or lost?"

She left her two-, five-, and six-year-old children at home.

There were no sitters, and there was no time to take her younger kids with her because it would be dark, and they would slow her down. She decided to leave them alone at the house with food and water. She would lock them inside, and they would be safe. She reluctantly left the house on horseback and traveled in the direction she thought that her daughters would be. After thirty minutes of looking, she found them. They told her a sheep had gone astray, so it had taken the extra time to retrieve it. Then they all trekked home together.

To her amazement, in her absence, she found that the young children had managed to get out of the house! My grandmother and her daughters looked around for them. They were able to find all but her rambunctious two-year-old little boy. My grandmother immediately thought of the worst-case scenario. There was a deep cliff a mile away from the house. She had her daughters tend the two little ones and headed on horseback to her nearest relative, telling them she needed help finding her son. Her relatives immediately went to get her husband.

My grandfather came back on horseback and rounded up all the people that he could to help him find his little boy. The Navajo community rallied together, searching for him until the sun came up to no avail.

At the first sign of morning light, the search party headed toward the cliffs. As they looked down the cliff, my grandparents saw the lifeless body of their little boy. He was laying on a ridge about fifty feet below. As my grandmother recounted the story, she had to catch her breath as tears streamed down her face. We were all distraught by what she had told us.

In those days, there was not a search and rescue team to call. Relatives and friends gathered, they tied ropes together, and carefully lowered my grandfather Shank down the canyon. He insisted on going down himself to retrieve his little boy. It was a risky call, but he did it. He grasped on to his son and brought him up.

This little boy was the uncle I never met. From my grandmother's perspective, he was her beautiful baby boy whom she loved like all her other children. His memory is embedded in her every waking day; she thinks of him daily and never will forget him.

At a time when I felt my life was hopeless, and I was in a deep depression, she told me, "We all feel pain at times. Whether rich or poor, of different races, different religions, man or woman, remember this: Our pain all feels the same because we are all the same, made of the same thread."

At that very moment, I had a wake-up call. Until then, I had it in my mind that my situation was far worse than anyone else's around me. I still have moments where I think my problems are the worst-case scenarios. In those moments, I think back to my grandmother's story. I am quickly reminded that I can handle life's detours. If she could handle it, I can, too; I'm part of her legacy, and I want to make her proud.

Hospital Visit

It was Wednesday, November 22, 2013. I remember receiving a diagnosis a couple of days earlier of H. Pylori, a bacterial stomach infection. The doctor prescribed me some heavy-duty antibiotics. I was resting at home until I began urinating blood and fevering. I didn't have anyone to take me to the hospital, and I thought I could be in trouble. I reluctantly drove myself to the emergency room in a daze. Fearful that I could be dying, I forced myself to trek outside my comfort zone.

I remember entering the hospital like a scared puppy. I looked up at the ceiling and said, "I can't do this anymore God, I'm tired, I give up."

I had a fever even though I was chugging down bottles of water. I was disoriented. Physically, I felt horrible. My ears were both clogged, I couldn't hear or swallow, and my throat was tight and raspy. My balance was off, and whenever I felt a fever come on, I tried to gulp water down.

Once admitted, the nursing staff gathered around me. They came in with a chest X-ray machine and took vials of blood and hooked me up to an IV. They did an EKG and could not figure out why my heart rate was very high, though I knew it was high because of previous anxiety-related experiences. They gave me a drip of antibiotics and morphine. After the drips finished, I asked to go to the restroom. To me, they all seemed very busy.

The nurse came in and unhooked me and said, "Are you sure you can go by yourself?"

I didn't know if I could do it, but I was going to try. I figured, "I'm in a hospital, if I pass out, it's the best place to be."

I stumbled my way to the restroom when something just overcame me. I was in deep desperation, mucus and blood draining from my body. I dropped to my knees in front of the latrine, faced the door, and said the "Our Father" prayer.

> *Our Father, Who art in heaven*
>
> *Hallowed be Thy Name.*
>
> *Thy kingdom come, Thy will be done,*
>
> *on earth as it is in heaven.*
>
> *Give us this day our daily bread,*
>
> *and forgive us our trespasses,*
>
> *as we forgive those who trespass against us;*
>
> *and lead us not into temptation,*
>
> *but deliver us from evil. Amen.*

Then, I recited the Hail Mary. From that point on, I believed that a divine holy miracle manifested itself. I was still feeling loopy and dazed, but I went into the restroom and the bleeding stopped. I heard a popping sound in my head; my ears suddenly unplugged, and I could hear again. Upon returning to my room, the doctor came in and told me the bleeding was probably caused by the H. Pylori infection. The staff gave me a beta blocker to lower my heart rate. I was informed my tests were all normal and that I had a viral infection.

When I walked into the hospital, I was in bad shape. After saying those prayers, I knew I was brought back from the brink of death to a sudden full bill of clean health.

The Release

A strange event happened after coming home from the hospital. It seemed all orchestrated by the Universe, at that very moment I was meant to come alive.

I call it my awakening.

The next morning following the hospital visit, I awakened to a strange, calm, heightened state of ascension. I'd woken up! I mean literally woken up! There was a tremendous surge of powerful energy circulating throughout my physical body. Calm, peace, and a *knowing* filled my spirit. Terms that I had never thought of before were looping in my thoughts.

"Stay in the present moment," the voice said.

Relevant information was downloaded throughout my system. I instinctively knew I was a writer and that my thoughts, ideas, and voice needed to be put in print.

My concept of time was extremely different as well. The past, present, and future were all intertwined. I was on a different plane; everything was crystal clear as though my human filter was removed. The first thought that came to my mind was that the veil had been lifted. My five senses were sharply heightened, so intense that I couldn't stand the smell of food. I sipped on water, not because I was thirsty, but because my human mind told me, "You haven't had any liquids, you need water to live."

Was I losing my mind? Going crazy?

I thought, "If this is losing it, I don't care, this feels incredible!"

Because regular food was overpowering, I couldn't even look at a piece of meat. I would look at a slab and I could sense the being that was killed. It broke my heart, and at the same time, it disgusted me. I had an unusual craving for sweet milk. I ended up opening a can of condensed milk and taking a few gulps.

It tasted amazing. It sustained me for the rest of the day. I eerily felt like a newborn baby. My skin was softer than usual, and it had a sweet smell to it. I smelled my breath; it smelled like a baby's. This gave me the impression that, in some cosmic way, I'd shed my physical body and was literally, somehow regenerated!

As I sat in my bedroom, time was nonexistent. (From my new understanding, it was a human, man-made concept, anyway.) I thought of my son and saw him as a baby, then I saw flickers of him playing sports, and briefly as a man. Pride swelled up within me;

he was going to be an amazing, good man. I closed my eyes, and if I thought of a person, I felt as if they were right there beside me. I felt their presence, their essence, their vibe. We were not separated by location; they were right there beside me. The distance my mind created was simply an illusion!

Everyone I loved and knew resided within me. I just had to imagine them, and their scent, aura, and image were right there with me!

"Life is nothing more than an experience," I was told. "You weren't brought forth to acquire gold, fortunes, or any physical items. That's foolish. You make your own blueprint; you make your own likeness, and it's perfect. You were born perfect, yet through programming, through the environment and the mundane tasks of everyday life, the memory of your perfection has been lost. You have perfectly placed connections, like pieces on a chessboard.

Some connections are a part of your life for the long term, others are a flicker in your life. Have you noticed? They have all taught you important life lessons. They've all been perfectly placed and manifested when you needed them for either assistance or to learn from them. How beautiful is that?"

Spirit spoke these truths into my head.

I closed my eyes, pictured my dad, and put my hands in front of me; an energy of strength, his garage scent mixed with the scent of Scope mouthwash was within arm's length. His sheer strong presence was before me. I was laughing and crying at the same time.

I opened my eyes, and nothing was there, and then his presence left. A thought came to my head, "You can't summon me yet, I have other work to do, please don't." These words transmitted to me, the idea of unspoken rules about the Spirit Realm and the Earthly Realm, which were not supposed to mix.

Vibrating at the highest level, I knew I was a spirit being of light, whose spirit was in existence for eons. I was light, I was darkness, I was nothing, yet I was everyone and everything all at once. I was already born, I had already died, yet I was also in the present moment all at once, and it was okay.

The house went eerily still. I didn't hear the hum of the refrigerator, or the creaking sound of the house settling in. I walked outside. It was awkwardly silent, just like the day the World Trade Center towers fell on 9/11. I walked to the corner of the street, and there was nobody around. I waited to see a bird, a plane; nothing.

Dogs weren't barking, not a sound. I couldn't spot a soul outside. I wasn't wearing a coat; the weather was perfect. The sun was radiantly shining. The message, "I am powerful, and I am a part of God," spoke to me.

"You are here to heal," it emanated.

I had no cares or worries. I was enthralled within the moment, the thought.

"All you have is this moment," was in the forefront of my mind.

The leaves outside seemed larger than usual; the veins oversized. It was like looking at human veins. Trees were like humans! The clouds billowed, and the colors were vivid and crisp. I had no hunger, no pain, and no attachments.

I went back into the house. My spirit was at peace, but my mind kept questioning this new altered state of being. I thought, "Should I be scared? Did I die and I don't know it?"

I turned on the TV for some type of human connection. Eight stations were available, and *Little House on the Prairie* was on one of them. The others were either infomercials or religious stations. The people on the television screen looked real, almost like I could reach through the screen and touch them.

I was suspended in time. It was comfortable, yet I was longing for my family to come back. I prayed that my mom and family would return home soon. As if on cue, my mom immediately walked in the door and glanced at me with concern. I looked at her, and I could read her mind. I could sense everything she was feeling. She was concerned for me. She came in and asked me if I was okay.

I naturally said, "Yes." After all, who comes out and says, "No, I'm having a fucked up, delusional episode, and I've been transmuted into an alternate reality."

Though I wondered why the neighborhood was empty, telling myself that "everyone was busy," I kept my voice of reason with me as much as I could. I had never felt such a disassociation from humans, yet at the same time sensed a strong unified connection with the Universe. Everything seemed interconnected with a balanced flow. The world was broken down into flowing energies. The feeling of excitement flowed quickly; the feeling of sadness moved slowly. Perfect energy moved at a normal steady pace.

In this heightened state, I could ask a question in my head, and an answer would visually pop up in my head.

I asked, "Have any other human beings been in this higher state of consciousness?"

In my mind, a picture of Michael Jackson appeared. I listened to one of his songs, and I swear my vocal cords were so flexible I could sing the song in his voice. I had complete control of every part of my body. My voice had the flexibility to be in any key I wanted. I was elated!

In this euphoric state, I learned about the flow of energy.

When I was in a depressive state, my energy slowed down to a snail-like pace, the world around me moving at a faster pace.

I was talking in my head to a higher power. I asked, "How does one get out of a depressive state?"

The higher thought told me to think of Christmas time, one of my favorite seasons. I visualized my mom's Christmas tree, I heard the music, and I smelled the pine tree. I thought of all my family members. I felt the energy and frequency of that state of being.

Instantly, I adjusted my mental and physical state of being into one of joy and love. I realized I would have to align and resync myself to match the pace of the outside world. With this sense came the strange ability to manipulate the energy around me.

I sat quietly and started manifesting excitement, which had an intense vibration, like molecules dancing. I manifested sadness, and the molecules seemed to slowly creep about, to almost nothing, no movement, no life.

While in the state of being in Spirit, I was the creator of my own environment. I kept intermittently thinking to myself, "This is not normal." I felt a deeper understanding of the Universe, yet also a great sense of isolation and dissociation from others.

I loved the feeling of peace, and the silence when walking outside. It was blissful yet at the same time unnatural. In this state, a feeling of needing to align emotionally and physically was the goal. Searching for a perfect balance for myself was what I was compelled to do. I was a being in the human realm, and spirits and angels were in the high vibrational spiritual realm. These were separate spaces, yet I found myself tinkering on a bridge.

I was existing partially in both realms!

I went into the shower, and I was unashamed of my nakedness. I found a voice saying, "This is your vessel. Isn't the human body beautiful?"

At that point, I almost forgot to put my clothes back on because it seemed so natural to possess such a miracle of life, a body. The feeling of being hot, cold, or in pain was not within my field. I felt invincible. All the feelings associated with shame and the forbiddances of nudity dissipated. It wasn't dirty or uncouth, it was a miracle and a gift of life; it was to be admired.

Spirit then relayed to me, "Humans put too much emphasis on labels, and this causes the human emotion of shame."

Nakedness was natural. At that same moment, I realized that our bodies are just like a plant, or a tree, and they should be hydrated, filled with sunlight, and exposed to kindness.

"Being good to oneself and others is how you grow," Spirit communicated.

Discarding Noise

The main task at hand when I walked into my cluttered bedroom was to discard all the noise and filter out all the distractions of my life.

I looked at my room and realized it was full of items and junk that I barely noticed or used. These items didn't nourish my soul in any way, shape, or form. I had clumped up old nail polish, headphones, and CDs I never listened to; the list went on and on.

That was my starting point; it was as if Spirit was encouraging me to dispose of items that no longer served me. The objects I had accumulated throughout the years were keeping me stagnant; they were my past, and I needed to be in the present. These items were holding me back in time.

I wondered if I would ever experience these past moments and emotions again? I thought I was truly happy at one point, but I couldn't have been because I wasn't my true self. I had fleeting moments of happiness, but I knew I was relying on someone else, rather than myself. I looked to my husband to provide me with inner and outer strength. We were emotionally connected, which was nice because I was lonely.

However, this new awareness that was being created wanted something different. I was willing to accept all my imperfections, all of my non-working choices, and most of all, I was confident standing in my own truth. This meant standing up for what I believed in, marching on my path alone, and being strong in times of weakness. The fiery radiating Aries within me could no longer hide in the shadows of darkness.

After cleaning the entire room, it felt bare yet fully equipped. The bag full of useless items was discarded. Discarding the past was bittersweet. *What if* thoughts came about as soon as I emptied the trash: "What if I need a number from the phones? What if the autographed items were worth money? What if I need the old medications?"

Ridiculous reasoning was going on within my mind. Then a message was sent telling me, "Be at peace with yourself, you did the right thing; move in the direction of your soul, your heart; leave behind what no longer serves you. Stay in the present moment, the past gives sadness, the future brings anxiety."

The thought "Better days are ahead" kept looping in my head.

While in the awakened state, the days were long, time stretched and expanded, which made sense, as I had so much to learn, like cramming for a big exam.

As I finished cleaning my cluttered past, the clock read noon. A garbage bag of my past was tossed away within half a day. I wasn't the least bit hungry, I didn't have breakfast, and I was fine. The few items that remained—the books that I had kept, the cross necklace, the book of my poems— were now of high importance. The items that were once meaningful were lost in all the clutter. I now had a sense of focus and direction. The noise and the distractions were taken away.

All the quotations I had saved over the last ten years were displayed in the forefront, taped on my wall. They all conveyed significant meaning and strongly resonated with me. Spirit communicated; these quotes were given to me for guidance. It said, these messages are sent daily to everyone, but people within the human realm are not paying attention with their blinders on. Start paying attention to the messages being relayed.

Among the quotations were:

"Downsizing material items allows one to focus on our true identity." – Thomas Merton

"Everything is perfect in the Universe—even your desire to improve it." – Wayne Dyer

"A musician must make music, an artist must paint, a poet must write if he is to be ultimately at peace with himself." – Abraham Maslow

"Courage is resistance to fear, mastery of fear, not absence of fear." – Mark Twain

I stuck some of the quotations next to my mirror, and while reading them, I glanced at the mirror. When I looked within the mirror, I could see an emanating light beaming around me, like an outline. "That must be my aura," I thought, as I stared at myself. I was beautiful, my smile was amazing, my teeth a dazzling white. While fixated on my image, I saw other amazing, beautiful forms morphing within the person staring back at me. I realized I existed within other people, and they were within me. Everyone was a perfect being yet not everyone had the realization of this. The thoughts within the mind were all that separated us. As souls, we were all mirrors of each other! I closed my eyes; I couldn't distinguish reality. Was I an angel? Again, I wondered if I was still alive as a human.

Looking at the mirror was mesmerizing and at the same time overwhelming. I quickly glanced away from the mirror to stop myself from freaking out.

The Shift

On the third day of my awakening, I was still dissociated from the rest of the world. My nine-year-old son came up to me with a concerned look in his eyes and said, "Are you really my mom?"

I smiled at him and told him, "She's still here."

There was a nudge from Spirit to talk about my struggles which would resonate with others. In the higher state, I could see projects from start to finish. I saw my husband getting better or continuing the drug use. I saw myself leave him, and I knew, no matter what, it would all turn out okay. I saw my child thriving, and I saw myself traveling without fear. I knew I had to get back to my human self. That evening, I took my sage out and saged myself and my room. "Spirit, I need whatever is guiding me to leave with love and so it is."

That night, I closed my eyes and said goodbye.

I awoke in the morning and felt like a piece of my soul had been ripped away. Like waking up after a hangover, empty and physically sick. I wasn't vibrating in a heightened state of awareness, and I was ravenously hungry. Life was now flowing at a slower pace, vibrating in a normal humdrum, mundane human state. It was as though the love of my life had been stripped away from me. I needed to find some Doritos and soda stat.

After munching down on a whole bag of chips and drinking three cans of cola, I reminisced about the miracle that had taken place. I was no longer fearful to the extent that I was before the awakening.

Do you know what I did in my newfound' anxiety-free state? I left my home, went to a Super Store, walked to the very back aisle, and felt alive again! Yes, I was no longer a prisoner of my own *mind*—I was set free! My body and powerful mind were healed; now it was time to pursue my passion of writing.

The Mind

A grappled mass of lustrous gray matter seemingly tangled and enmeshed.

A masterpiece of a jewel; encased in bone, outlined within a sea of flesh.

Some decorate within the ordinary, others with flamboyance and grace.

In one may loom a fresco painting; in another, a simplistic smiley face.

Within dreams is where hidden meanings and deep fantasies hide.

Where logic is non-existent, and consciousness subsides.

The mind is programmed to be separate; individual, to live life numb.

The time is now, the place is here, to heal, to experience; to feel as one.

My Intuition

From an early age, I've always had vivid, colorful, scentful dreams. The very first dream I can recall involved colors, sounds, and primordial feelings. I could see myself as a zipping charge of light energy.

Around the first year of working for Head Start, fresh out of college, I did a dream log. If a friend was having a difficult time, I would have a vivid dream about the entire scenario. This part of myself was always hard for me to express to strangers or to people who didn't know me. The response has always been polarized.

I receive messages from my spirit guides

through sensory communication, called clairsentient, and through visual messages called clairvoyance. I am shown symbols about births, deaths, and future incidents. The only way I can explain it is if I concentrate on a person, I will then dream about them. I am shown a path that most likely they will follow because it's part of their programming. However, because of free will, they may or may not choose to follow the engrained path.

When I disclose my dreams about someone, most are relieved that someone understands them, and they divulge everything about their situation. In my mind, I become a listening ear and a source of encouragement for them.

At other times, it has gone bad; the dead-cold stare and awkward silence tell me they are not ready. Or they think I'm trying to trick them. When I sense this, from that point on, I shut my mouth and never mention it again.

I believe in past lives, and I am sure that I've had this ability in another lifetime. I also know I was sought out and harmed because of it.

A past life memory I have is of living by a seaport with people who looked like Quakers. There was a recollection of being drowned in water. I am not afraid of water, I love water, but I don't like having my eyes or head covered. My fear of suffocation is present now because of the past life trauma of being drowned. I am presently working through releasing the trauma. I release by visualizing the scene and assuring myself, you are safe, I am here with you, this is only a mere moment. Your true self is safe. I then see myself as set free and released from the mere moment of tragedy.

It's been a learning experience on how to manage and embrace the clairvoyant part of me, which was enhanced after the awakening. I am learning about a code of ethics, which makes so much sense. Now when I dream about someone, I ask for their permission before I share the information. When receptive, I reveal what I see. If they are not ready, I move on.

I've been able to further explore the realm of the dream world. I know how to lucid dream. Lucid dreaming is a state where you are aware within the dream state that you are dreaming. You can touch, taste, feel, and smell in the dream world. I have explored astral travel, where you can travel to other galaxies, and other dimensions. If you are in a well state of being, it can open new perspectives; however, if you are in a challenging space, the dimension could bring about confusion and distortion.

Aha Moment

I had a series of profound aha moments after my awakening. I listened to spiritual teacher Darius M. Barazandeh's, "You Wealth Revolution" podcast.

There was a gentleman on his show who said, "Think of the person who has done you the most wrong in your life."

I immediately thought of my son's dad.

Then he said, "Now picture that person telling you what you want to hear from them."

I thought to myself, "There is nothing I want to hear from him. I want him to move into action and for him to act upon the things he says he's going to do. His words are useless to me." I sat there thinking, "This man is full of shit, he's not helping me, this is bullshit."

I kept listening. Then a caller came on and explained how she was in a deep depression because she was separated from her cat. She said she had owned the cat for ten years and that it was the love of her life. She had to move to an apartment for financial reasons, and her cat wasn't allowed to stay. She gave her cat to another family temporarily.

What the gentleman said next was profound: "The cat isn't the love of your life. The idea of love comes from within you, not from your cat. You're the one manifesting that love. But you made up your mind that it's the cat bringing it to you, and it isn't true. You are in control of how you feel; you're bringing the love into your life; it's not coming from the cat."

I realized how this idea related to my

situation.

The reason I wasn't making any progress with leaving my son's dad was because I had an idea embedded in me of having a perfect union. In my mind, I thought he could quickly overcome his addiction to pain pills. I thought of addiction like a light switch. In my head, I thought it was a choice that he could easily change.

The example that I was holding on to was my mom and dad's marriage. They worked together as a team, and when one faltered, the other one would step up. They rarely argued, and when they did, it was constructive, and they never went to bed without saying they were sorry. My dad rarely raised his voice to my mother, and I never heard him utter any words of disrespect to her. I, therefore, had expectations that I would be treated in this manner.

When my husband and I first married, we

seemed idealistically perfect for each other. We were both working full time, and we communicated well. Once drugs were introduced, our relationship was mainly nights worrying about his whereabouts and days spent worrying about where the money in our bank account was going. The whole time I was holding on to an idea that I could change him. I tried guilting him to break his habit, telling him, "If you love your son and me, you will quit."

He loved us, but I don't doubt that the drug had an extreme hold on him. If he didn't have his OxyContin for the day, he would profusely sweat, vomit, and have diarrhea. It was as though he'd caught a severe case of the flu; but once he popped that pill in his mouth, the symptoms vanished, and he was normal again.

The epiphany of the podcast allowed me to look at my turbulent relationship with my mother. I've held on to an idea of how I think she should interact with me. My idea of a mother is that she should always be supportive, encouraging, and nurturing. My made-up image. The truth is my mom is a realist and a woman of high expectations. I can never live up to the daughter she pictures and wants me to be, but I accept her view of me, and I accept who she is.

Even though it would be nice to hear an encouraging "You can do it! Go for it" attitude, I know the response I'm going to get. "Are you sure? What if it doesn't work out?" is what I'm going to get. My mother's way of raising me is one of the reasons I have second-guessed myself in the past. I wanted a hug at times when I was down, but I couldn't approach her like that. At times of despair, I wondered if my biological mother would have hugged me? I made up a fantasy in my head of my biological mother being proud of me, and it would temporarily cheer me up.

Another profound aha moment came when I took a self-improvement class. A girl in her late twenties named Jackie stood up and said, "I really miss my grandma and haven't spoken to her in eight years."

She explained that her parents were addicts, and her grandmother had raised her since she was nine years old. Then when she turned fourteen, her grandmother let her drug addict mom stay at the house. Jackie was appalled! How could her grandma let a drug addict in the house? Jackie told herself her grandma didn't love her, and she moved out of the house. The trainer asked, "When your grandma let your drug-addict mom move in with you, what percent of love do you think she had for you?

Jackie said, "Ten percent."

Trainer: "You know for sure her love towards you was ten percent?"

Jackie: "No, I don't, but I made that up in my

head."

Trainer: "What if your grandma still loved you one hundred percent, and you made it up that she only loved you ten percent; is that possible?

Jackie: "That is a complete possibility, of course. My grandmother is going to still love her daughter who is my mom, and of course, she can still love me, too."

Jackie: "I'm calling my grandma to tell her I miss her."

Jackie went on break and called her grandmother. Her grandmother told her, "I felt you'd distanced yourself from me. I have never stopped loving you."

After this experience, I realized how I've been withholding my love from others. Especially in times when I didn't feel my love was reciprocated. I would build an imaginary wall. The good thing is I am the one who built the wall, and I am the one who

SHELL SILVERSMITH

can tear it down.

Quantum Healer

I was sick with stomach aches and a nauseous feeling for a month in 2016. In desperation, I purchased a healing session with a quantum healer. I forgot about the session until Sunday night when I received an email saying, "You have a telephone appointment at 1:00 p.m. tomorrow."

The controlling part of my personality realized I knew nothing about this lady. In a last-minute attempt, I started reading all I could about this person. Her reviews were good, and her work was relevant. I concluded she was a legitimate healer. I went to bed at 11:00 p.m. that night and awoke at

3:00 a.m., which was odd for me because I usually sleep through the night. I know this is too much info, but I had a bowel movement and went back to bed, then I had three more before the session and I thought, "This is odd, it's not normal for me."

I also took my son to school, and as I was walking into his school, which was in a Catholic Church, the lights where Father entered the church were flickering. I had never noticed that before. I stopped and stared at the flickering lights, and a raven flew over my head. At lunchtime, I went to a sandwich shop, and on my way out, there was a group of crows in the street.

I thought, "This is odd." I went home, and as soon as I stepped into my doorway, she called.

She introduced herself. She was warm and inviting. She explained that angels were called upon to heal my ailments. She then said, "I summoned Saint Raphael at 3:00 a.m.

this morning."

I told her that's when I suddenly woke up.

She said, "Yes, you're being worked on. Have you noticed any birds around, like a raven or a crow?"

I said, "Yes."

"Those are your guides, and they will appear to you in that form." Then she asked me some questions about my childhood, and I told her I was really close to my dad, and he'd passed. Just then, my left hand started twitching.

Then she said, "He says he's holding your hand right now."

I looked to my left. I wanted to see him, but I couldn't; but when I closed my eyes, I felt him. His strength, his scent, and his spirit were next to me.

Then she said, "Something happened to you as a little girl that scared you at eleven years of age; we're going to heal that."

The only event at age eleven that scared me was when my dad's friend flipped his jeep coming home from work and he died. I remember seeing the sadness on his daughter's face. She was the same age as me. I remember going to the funeral, and it jarred me how fragile life is. From that point on, I had a fear of losing my dad. This feeling was constant. When I did lose him, it shattered me. She claimed to have taken that fear out of me. I felt my heart twitching when she was doing this, and it was so odd, but I believe she did help me. She then said something confusing to me over the phone, while still on the call.

"Your dad has left; I am seeing a woman in white. She looks Native American. I feel she is telling me she won't ever leave you again. She is making a motion like she is cradling a baby."

"I'm taking care of the baby, is what I sense

she is communicating to me. She's there with you. Could this be your grandmother or your mom?"

"No, they are all alive," I tell her.

"Do you know who she is?" the healer questions. She ends with, "Your guides have told me that you have very big fish to fry."

In my mind, she was the gypsy I had dreamed of earlier, she was wise, an old soul, a shaman.

Even though I have had psychic abilities about other people, I was still skeptical. I looked for loopholes and discrepancies; I half-heartedly believed her. The session ended, and for the rest of the day, I felt my guides surrounding me. I was perplexed as to who the woman could be. Why did she have a baby? Maybe the healer was mistaken, or it could have been a fluke?

I quickly dismissed what she had told me.

Self-Reflection

When I lived in the house with the white picket fence and had financial abundance, I found myself going through the daily motions of life. There were no thoughts of my heritage, and prayers were obsolete. My thoughts were solely on me and everything within my little bubble. I was in isolation, wondering how I could get ahead financially. I had steps laid out in my head of how I could thrive. My greatest dilemma of the day was, do I want a mocha latte or chai tea? How do I make a Jell-O salad for the neighborhood barbecue?

My connections were with those who

mirrored my life. It was as though I was on a treadmill, and I had no time for anything that didn't fit my mold or anyone that didn't align with my happy life. This was on a subconscious level at the time, not being fully aware of my narrow-minded thinking. I knew I loved my family; I knew I loved others, but I didn't have a true sense of an authentic self-identity.

I created sacred moments of my own. I did the Wayne Dyer meditation on YouTube, "I am." I can't tell you the number of times I've been on the verge of a panic attack, and I concentrated on the tones and the mantra of the track. It transported me to another place, one of tranquility and calm.

When I meditated in the park for the first time, I was self-conscious about who would be watching me. Then I started showing up every day. Meditation brought me *at one* with nature, the trees, leaves, and sky all imprinting themselves within my unique operating system. It was liberating and helped me align. I needed a reboot because it was easy to lose sight of myself in day-to-day life.

The realization that I'm running my own race is a hard one for me to come to terms with. I tend to look at other people in life and measure my success against theirs. In my family, there are wonderful cooks; unfortunately, I'm not one of them. Chopping celery and growing tomatoes are not something I get enjoyment out of. Some skills will never align with me, and it's okay.

I sleep with a basketball next to my bed. I love the feel of a basketball in my hand. I love bouncing the ball and releasing it from my hand into the hoop. I feel alive. I watch every Utah Jazz basketball game and love my Utah Utes.

I coach a boys' basketball team; coaching them brings me pure joy. Through basketball, we learn about commitment, goal setting, and determination.

A pastime of mine was to stand in old libraries or bookstores. I enjoyed the smell and the historical energy stored in the vast cubicles of knowledge. In coffee shops, I "people watched," browsed through my computer, and took in the slow energy. Being at a summer *pow wow*, with a fire going, the drums beating, elders, women, and children dancing around the fire in unison is heaven. Seeing the flicker of the flame on my grandmother's smiling face— it's those moments where I am alive.

What may get my endorphins pumping may do nothing for another person. It's getting a little easier, walking to the beat of my own drum with acceptance and pride.

I am also coming to terms with my inner guilt. I can't fluently speak my native language, Navajo. I understand and speak small phrases, but I cannot hold a conversation.

Because I was raised in the suburbs of Salt Lake City, I only knew one other Navajo girl in elementary school, and she was shy and didn't talk to anyone. I had one other Navajo friend in high school, and she didn't know how to speak Navajo either. I have learned phrases and words on the internet and by listening to family.

I asked questions and tried to speak the language when I visited the reservation. I traveled there on average twice a year and learning to speak Navajo has been a difficult task. For financial reasons, I couldn't drop everything and live on the reservation to learn. Also, the dialect and pronunciation are different from anything I've ever heard. I accept that I did not learn it completely, and I know if I do learn it fluently, it will be something I've worked extra hard at attaining, even harder than earning a college degree.

I've always put writing last, and I've laid in

bed at night, wondering, "Why didn't I write today?" Then I list the excuses one by one in my head. One of them is, "Nothing may come out of it." However, for me, writing this book has been cathartic. I have let go of all my expectations and the book just is.

Before, I would tell myself, "Shell, you need to be more like Shakespeare, Grisham, Hawthorne, or Blume, all your writing heroes." Now, I know there never has and never will be another writer like them. On the same token, there will never be another one like me either.

As I become emotionally stronger, and physically stronger by working out at the gym, there is a shift taking place. I now find myself asking, "How did you put up with so much crap?" I also realize how I've been talking to myself in my head. I find I'm always scolding myself and never praising myself. I am now counteracting my harsh words with kind, loving words, and I treat myself to massages and long walks, and periodic naps. I tell my body and mind, "Thank you for being here, thank you for your service, I love you," and then comes the shift.

Self-Discovery

With this new self-discovery, I notice how my masculine energy is higher than my feminine energy. I attribute it to growing up around all boys and being an Aries. I decided to explore wearing makeup and dressing more feminine. I'm not ready to hang with a completely girly girl yet, though; that is an emergency last resort.

I tried emanating a softer female side, and let's just say I put in a lot of effort. It felt good, but it took extra time. I put on a skirt, glued some uneven eyelashes on, and received some free things, LOL. I went to the local gas station and refilled my drink. The guy smiled and said, "Sweetheart, you don't have to pay for that." Maybe I've found the real secret to the Universe?

Doors were opened quickly for me, instead of being slammed in my face. The feminine energy has its own power, and I'll admit, it's nice. The downfall is my eyes were irritated by the glue from the eyelashes, and wearing a skirt was a challenge. I've decided on a happy medium; I'll put on makeup and wear my earrings and bracelet, that's more like me.

I'm also digging deep into this anxiety thing. I'm truly wondering if it's something attached to my childhood. Or if it's hormonal? I know the thoughts that trigger it. Whenever I have the thought, "I can't breathe," it's triggered.

For instance, it's been hitting 100 degrees. I see people driving around in it. I tell myself that I'm not letting the heat stop me. Even though the windows are down, it's the heat hitting my face and the feeling of not getting any air, although it's far from the truth. I've forced myself to go through it by pouring water on my head, drinking water, and telling myself, "Do you want to set a bad example for your son?" Then once I'm going and, on my way, it somehow becomes easier. Once I reach my destination, I'm fine. It's the initial leaving and the getting there that is difficult. Once I've reached where I need to be, it's like a switch, and I'm fine. That right there tells me it's a mental issue.

What am I doing to overcome this obstacle?

I'm forcing myself to do things I don't want to do.

I went to the county landfill last week. I thought to myself, "Where is a place I don't want to be? Where is a place that I could not stand to be?"

The dump. I set out early in the morning. It took me twenty minutes to get there in light traffic. Once I got there, I said, "Can I drive through? I'm looking for someone."

They said, "Yes."

There I was in a smelly dump. Many workers were there, and I looked around, stopped, and got out. The smell hit me hard, and I hurried back into my car. I sat looking at the vast wasteland, looked for the exit, and made myself sit with the discomfort.

I asked myself, "What is your fear about this place?"

"Getting trapped, not being able to breathe, getting lost in all the waste."

"Look at the scenery, do you fear it?"

I looked at all the men working around in it, just going about their business. I saw seagulls flying around, and I looked at the trash being dumped. It had some interesting things about it. Now I don't fear landfills. I drove out, thinking how silly I had been with my thoughts about landfills. I drove away feeling accomplished.

What are your fears? Elevators? Clowns? Snakes? Can you find a way to confront your fear? I would admire you if you tried…and if you failed? The fact that you set forth and tried would be something to celebrate.

The Universe, in its own way, forced me to write today. I've been going to the gym, going out a little more, and in the process, I've been neglecting my writing.

Late at night, while walking down the stairs, my knee suddenly locked. I hobbled around with an ice pack. I was forced to be still, to sit down and write. In the back of my mind, I'm thinking that my life isn't perfectly put together.

Part of me thinks, how can I have great advice when I am somewhat broken?

Another part of me is saying, "One day, you're going to be in a much better place, and there will be people who need to know you went through the darkness and made it to the light on the other side."

I can envision life getting better, and for me that would be waking up and being excited for the next day. Right now, I'm still at the point of, "How am I going to get through today?" My favorite thing to do is to wake up and start my day by going to the park and walking. I listen to the sounds of nature, look at the clouds, and sometimes I meditate.

I am looking forward to better days, where I can pick up and travel, and connect with people, but for now, I'm right where I need to be.

In Poverty

I live in one of the poorest neighborhoods in the city. It doesn't feel unsafe, or drug riddled, even though I've seen proof of it. I've made connections with some of the neighbors. Yes, some are undocumented, and some are using drugs and alcohol. Even though the outside of where I live is disheveled, I try to maintain a positive appearance on the inside of my home. I work to keep the dishes washed, clothes clean, plants watered, the little things.

One day I watched a sad-looking teenager walk out of the library. She was wearing jeans and a T-shirt and carried a beat-up backpack. Yet, she had a handful of books. I said a prayer for her; I said, "Please bless her with greatness, Lord. She could be struggling, yet she chooses to read and is probably a good student."

When I substitute in classrooms, it's inspiring to see students who probably have nothing at home, yet they choose to listen and excel in the classroom. That is something I wish was instilled in all of us—excelling even though some of us have great disadvantages. Last night, a helicopter was flying around our apartment, looking for a lawbreaker.

There are two neighbors in the unit by us who are constantly screaming at each other; their kids run outside holding on to each other. The place is trashy, and I clean up around the dumpsters every day. A few hours later it looks just as it did before I cleaned up.

Do the people throwing trash around have any pride?

But when I think about it, they are working a minimum wage job, barely making it, and they feel stuck, trapped. The last thing they care about is where they are throwing their garbage. The mom, who was probably beaten the night before, comes out and is smoking; she's in survival mode.

I've put myself here, though I can't imagine living here in five years. For now, it's my home, and I accept it. People regularly buy drugs out in the open in this environment.

Our neighbor is a nice guy, but he's struggling with addiction. He keeps losing his job. I heard him fighting with someone over the weekend—a fight over meth. He has children, and I look at them and pray, "God, let these kids overcome."

There is a neighbor lady who knocks on my door to sell me tamales at midnight. I tell her it's too late, and she smiles and is back a couple of nights later. Some random guy asks me if I want to buy some items:

watches, coins, and jewelry. I think to myself, "These are stolen." Someone in a white Cadillac is pounding on our door at 4:00 a.m.; I don't answer and talk to the neighbors the next day. They conclude that they must have had the wrong unit.

My neighbors are of a low socioeconomic class; a lot of them are laborers, and others don't work. I find that they all want the best for their kids, they all want a better life, and some are stuck in habits they don't know how to get out of. I do know that a lot of them wouldn't hesitate to loan me an egg or help me if I needed to move furniture. I don't know how long we will live here, but I know it's taught me a lot about living in survival mode.

I've been blessed; I haven't had a drug addiction. I've watched people I love die of alcoholism, and I'm currently watching family members battling various drug addictions. I don't have the answers to how they can quit the debilitating habit. I know the decision to stop must become a strong conviction from within. Unfortunately, it usually takes something bad happening to come to that realization.

Addiction, in all its forms, can corrupt the soul. I admit I love alcohol. I won't turn down a dark hoppy beer; I could literally drink one every day. A glass of wine at night is soothing to my soul, but since I know it could be my downfall, I only drink on holidays and in moderation.

I've been through phases where I've become addicted to social media on the internet. I used to spend as much as five hours a day scrolling through Twitter and Facebook. I have cut my time down to an hour a day. It's an addiction, and the sad thing is the more outrageous the post, the more attention it garners. I figure if I spend five hours a day nurturing my own body and soul, I could make great progress.

I think the social media posts were a way for me to live vicariously through others. It was interesting to see the places others have traveled, and the food they ate, instead of looking at myself and my own real life. I'm not glamorous. The real Shell (my nickname for Rachelle) frequents libraries, attends lectures, *pow wows*, and is a bad cook.

There are *pow wow* songs that I keep listening to because they remind me of being at my Grandpa Smith's house in New Mexico and hearing him sing.

My *shináli* (paternal grandpa) left us too soon, but his spirit was very influential to me, just pure goodness and hard work that embodied him and my dad. That's why, lately, I have been getting up early, and I've been keeping my house clean because if my house is dirty, it feels like I'm dishonoring my dad and grandpa. My dad disliked me sleeping past 10:00 a.m. He would literally pound on my door and tell me I was wasting the day away. I didn't get it then; I do now. When I wake up now, I know today is a blessing, even when there are difficult responsibilities ahead. I intend to make the most of my day in a way that is meaningful to me and those around me.

My Gift

In my mind, there is a romanticized view of what it's like to write a novel. I've always pictured writers being in the mountains or a large tidy office. To me, the successful ones have a beautiful office filled with classic literature, typing away on their expensive, powerful laptop.

Yet, the reality for me is different. I get most of my writing done at the public library or the park if my battery permits. Right now, my oasis is a local park. It's a place to meditate, walk, people watch; it has everything I need. I'm grateful that I have the bare minimum, it makes for fewer distractions. If I had more money, I know I would be wasting my time driving to a sushi bar across town, and I wouldn't get to my writing. Or if I had the money to buy a new outfit, I'd also need the accessories, and the list becomes endless.

When I am at my happiest, I also face some of my greatest challenges. I've had two panic attacks, and I usually run home when this happens. This time, I did something completely different. I focused on completing the task at hand, in conjunction with slowing down my breathing.

I was on the third floor of a building, and I thought, "Nobody is here, and if I get stuck, nobody will know."

I believe this thought triggered my panic.

"What if I get stuck in the elevator?" I thought next.

It spiraled down from there. I became dizzy

and looked for the quickest exit. I was able to get down to the main floor. I went outside and closed my eyes until I calmed down.

I forced myself to go back in, and I found a receptionist to answer my questions. As soon as I started talking to her, my panic immediately subsided. It's so mind boggling to think that a mere thought triggered my panic. I've made up my mind that if I am on a mission, such as going to a store or going to an appointment, I won't abandon what I've started. If I do, it then becomes a pattern.

This appointment had a positive outcome. Before this experience, I would abort the mission, and it would make me feel worse for leaving. I've learned to cope with my body and the feelings that happen with panic, but I can't handle the feeling of failure if I don't follow through.

I understand people who have a difficult time getting out socially, going to weddings, or going out in busy crowded places. I can relate to the feeling of giving a public speech in front of hundreds of people. The mere thought of having to do this humongous task can send a lot of people into a panic.

For some, even though it seems minimal, these small tasks can become a great ordeal. At one point in my life, I spent most of my time making up excuses as to why I couldn't attend a social gathering. I might have a panic attack in the middle of the event, for example.

However, coming up with excuses and lying is not in my character. Now that the truth has come out, I am attending some events, even if it means I endure anxiety.

What is strange about my situation is, if I am given a topic to talk about in front of an audience, I can do it! I feel comfortable in front of a group of people. I enjoy public speaking. If the subject has meaning to me and I am given time to prepare, it turns out amazing.

I have made small changes that are positively affecting my life. I am learning that taking small steps is better than not taking any at all. I am no longer running from confrontation. I do the difficult task of confronting, and sometimes the situation gets resolved, and that's the best feeling. Sometimes resolution doesn't come, but deep down I know I tried.

I'm also starting something new. I have been listening to podcasts about manifestation. So now, before I go to bed, I visualize how I want tomorrow to go. I mostly see myself writing and meditating. I even visualize a nice clean book cover, and I hold my book with a sense of accomplishment. I will eventually do something I learned from a random podcast, where you record yourself talking as if you've already accomplished all you set out to do in life. I have started my path to manifestation.

Self-Acceptance

Another new hobby I began is working out at the gym. After three months, I wasn't seeing the results I wanted. I thought about quitting. It's now been eight months of going to the gym for an hour a day, and I am fifteen pounds lighter and have a shrinking tummy.

Why didn't I do this sooner?

The hardest part is changing how I eat. It takes me twice as long to get ready in the morning because I must prepare meals for not only breakfast but lunch too. I am hoping soon this preparation time will become second nature, and I'll get faster at it. Exercising at first felt like work and a job;

now it's my escape, it's my stress reliever, my time block.

Working on getting still and being able to focus on inner goals is something I am consciously doing. I get quiet, turn off my phone and electronic devices for twenty minutes, or listen to a daily meditation—Wayne Dyer, Deepak Chopra, and Marisa Peer to name a few. Meditation clears my mind and gives me a reset, especially when I have trouble looping in my mind.

I start my day by writing down the three most important tasks for the day. I start the first project and stay with it until completion. If I can't finish the task, I write it down and start on it the next day. It's difficult for me to follow through because it's easy to get interrupted and distracted. I stick to task number one and follow it through until completion; two and three are more optional. I complete all tasks before I write down a new one.

I tend to start new projects, and they never reach completion, especially with writing. I've started at least ten novels, reached the halfway point, and either lost interest or felt the relevance had disappeared. Maybe one day I will complete some of them, maybe they will be forever lost. The hard part is I have poured my heart and soul into these writings, so I realize I can't just abandon them anymore.

I am no longer ashamed of who I am or who I am becoming. Growing up, people in the city would always ask me, "Are you Navajo?"

Some people have this stereotype of me already in their mind, and say, "Oh, you must be a foster child," or "You live off government money your tribe gets paid." Others have simply had bad experiences.

"We went to a reservation, but we only saw a lot of drunk people who asked us for money."

Then you get the opposite, "My friend took me to the reservation, it was the most spiritual experience," or "I had a Navajo friend; they made the best Navajo tacos and beautiful rugs and jewelry."

When I went to the reservation, there would be a set of rules from my parents: You shake hands with everyone; you can't wear shorts that are too high up; if you see a dust devil, walk away from it, it's bad luck. When we were served dinner, I had to let Grandma and all the aunties go first and so on. I understand a lot of Navajo, but I can't speak it back. I've always been afraid of someone talking to me in Navajo and not being able to communicate it back. If that happened, there would be someone there to help translate for me.

Now, I am who I am. I am a Navajo who lives in the city, who listens to *pow wow* music and Tash Sultana, and watches Gaia TV. I am a Navajo who enjoys an ice-cold hoppy beer, See's candy suckers, and has a gift with words. Who I am can't be put into a square box, labeled, or categorized. That's what makes life beautiful. We are all unique, different, yet all interconnected to everything imagined or unimagined.

I have befriended some people who have illnesses that they will never recover from, and they are young. When I interact with them, I want them to forget about their illness, if only for a moment. If they want to vent, curse, or cry, I am there. Inside, I want to take away their suffering. They are the brave ones; they have been forced to look for that sense of inner peace while looking into the face of despair.

I look at my own days of despair and realize that life moves forward. If I've had a bad day, it's so easy to give up, to throw in the towel, get an ice cream shake, sit in front of the TV, and check out. What's hard is getting up, going to the gym, eating right, and saying

"I'm sorry" when I know I'm wrong.

Taking ownership, even when I don't feel like it, that's bravery.

Fears

Plagued with anxiety, I've had to search deep within to try and understand the root cause of all my symptoms.

One evening, I was about to go to dinner and couldn't get on the freeway. As I approached the freeway entrance, my palms began to sweat, I had a fast heartbeat, then dizziness. I ended up turning around and felt defeated, ashamed, and back at square one again. I went home and meditated and prayed. I had thoughts of, "How can you do this to yourself? Do you want to live or just exist?"

I felt horrible about myself. Then, a couple of hours later, I heard numerous sirens coming from the next street. I walked around the corner and could hear people gathering outside. "He bolted in front of an oncoming car," someone said.

People were outside gawking, and the police were swarming the place, blocking off the road. They carted off the man on a stretcher. My thoughts were, "I hope he doesn't die." I spent the rest of the night in self-reflection about my life. I concluded that my senses had detected danger was lurking in the vicinity, which in turn triggered my panic.

The next morning, I went to the gym and saw a man that I'd known for five years. He prays at the cathedral every day and carries a Bible around. He texts scriptures to me by phone every now and then. He is a single father who once had a bad drug addiction when he was younger, but he has since turned his life around. We started talking, and he told me he had a financial crisis and was barely able to turn it around.

FINDING MY SACRED

He asked, "How are you?"

I told him the truth. "Life is good and a blessing, but I struggle with anxiety."

Then he asked me, "Are you truly being you? Are you doing what you need to do every day for your good? I'm not a doctor, but something is obviously weighing you down."

At that moment, I felt a bit lighter.

Truth is, I think I am doing everything I know how to do for myself. But even the small things are part of my weight. For instance, within this past year, I went back to my ex. He is still legally my husband, and he is still an addict and always will be. My son tells me, "Mom, I want you and Dad together."

His dad tells me, "We are married and that means through thick and thin. I will never love another person as much as I love you." Yet he drinks, smokes, and brings home a paycheck. I've been in denial. I've been an accomplice, buying him beer, allowing him to leave his weed pipe here and there. Thinking, if it's hidden, nobody knows; it's our secret. Yet my soul knows.

Today I urged him to stop and get some help. He says he believes it is time to quit, and he is willing to try.

While he's working on himself, I also have a lot of work to do on myself, starting with little things. It's a blessing to be able to exercise, pray every day, and visualize. Next, I'd like to donate to charities, study my roots, and concentrate on family and finances. I intend to be better and do better than the day before.

I watched a Wayne Dyer video in which he talked about physical pain and how it is connected to our emotional pain. Looking inward, I realize I have created a story about myself. Looking deep into my core, trust in myself is lacking. I am always second-guessing myself and feeling like an imposter.

To counteract these feelings and old stories, there was meditation, therapy, and hypnosis, all of which were explored. As I did something called EFT tapping, thoughts of my mom came up. She was always telling me, "It's not good enough."

I have told myself, "I will not let my mother dictate the direction I want to go in. I will welcome her advice, but I will not automatically do what she thinks or feels is right for me". I love her dearly, but her influence (while most of it has been positive) and some of her words have hindered my growth because I have allowed them to.

What brings joy to my heart?

Seeing my grandmother and being in her presence. She is sheer power, innocence, love, and strength all rolled into one. It's scary right now to think of how much influence she has had on me; I would do anything for her.

I try not to let my mind go to when she can no longer be here. When it comes, I hope she goes in peace, and I hope I am mentally and physically prepared for it. My other fear is I don't want to see my mother decline. She is a strong, confident woman, and I want her to always have that inner and outer strength.

Energy & Frequency

I used to believe that my panic attacks were triggered by outside factors. However, I know that I am the one causing my distress by allowing my negative thoughts to become a runaway train. I am uncomfortable when out in a crowd and may always be a little apprehensive. Unknown territory is tough for me to navigate, but I can now shorten the panic and mentally calm myself down faster.

To me, that's a victory. My next step is to see if I can completely control all of my thoughts. That is a goal of mine. To no longer let my fear escalate to where it feels out of my control. I am no longer avoiding difficult confrontations or difficult matters in general. I tackle the most difficult tasks first. I'm pushing myself to get out, and some days are harder than others. I know my new habits can become my downfall or a new blessing.

I am being tested. These troubles, all the issues, the hurt, the pain, and the uncertainty, have forced me to become mentally stronger. I accept all that has happened to me and take responsibility for all my actions and reactions, and I accept this wholeheartedly; it's what is.

I look at the world in terms of energy and frequencies. I intend to reach an energy and frequency level that is as high as I can attain. In return, I can be in tune with my higher self and other high-emitting energies. I am reinventing myself. No longer a victim with intense feelings of hurt. No longer holding on to anger with feelings of revenge. No longer sad with tears of pain. No longer helpless and looking outside myself for others to rescue me. I am now wide open, and free like a vast ocean.

I've heard that when one is trying to improve, trying to change for the better, one will encounter a great force of resistance. I'm experiencing this right now. My car was sideswiped, my spouse complained about how I am not substituting in school, and he doesn't want to have the whole financial responsibility. I've worked since I turned fourteen, and I don't want to find myself in my dad's shoes. In my session with the quantum healer, she relayed the message he had for me from beyond. This healer knew nothing about my dad, yet she had this message from him, where he said, "I worked myself to death."

How many of us are working ourselves to death? I would estimate a great many of us are. To pay the basic expenses of living, adding the luxuries of cable, cell phones, and the internet, you're stuck in the daily grind. I'm giving myself six months of trying this writing thing, and if it pans out, then I've found my calling. If it doesn't, I will continue to do it on the side and hope someone will find meaning within my words.

It's been a couple of weeks since I last wrote because things have gone from bad to worse. I've been in bed the last three days with a flu bug, body aches, fever, sore throat, and just a severe tired feeling. Today, I had just enough energy to do a load of laundry. Then as I lay in bed, I let my thoughts go to the worst possible places ever. I thought, what if I lose my mom? What if I don't recover? What if this is the best I can do in life?

Am I enough? As I was crying and on the verge of a meltdown, an inner voice said, "Get it together!"

I know being down on myself is serious because I've been in a depressive state before. I remember going to the doctor, and he didn't help me much, but my therapist did. I let my thoughts take over, and I'm good at beating myself up. In some cases, it has been a motivator, but it's also taken a toll on me.

I did some EFT tapping with Nick Ortner and found online meditations with Wayne Dyer. They are helpful resources; however, it's me who has to take the initiative to heal myself. Nobody can fight harder than I can for me, and I will say, I know I'm worth the sacrifices and efforts.

I'm still sick, but I am slowly getting better. Even though I have a list of tasks to get done, I have thrown the list aside and I am concentrating on the basics: keeping hydrated, getting my rest, and trying to eat. During these times, when I am alone with my bedroom door closed, I am isolated. I am left alone with only my thoughts. Today, I purposely let my thoughts go to good times and good places, imagining great outcomes. I sat in bliss with them for about twenty minutes, then my family started knocking on my door.

Thinking positively takes work, because it's foreign to me, imagining good outcomes, recalling good times. But in the end, I had a smile on my face and joy within my heart. I am wondering if I can keep the pattern going? Can I make it into a habit? I am going to have to work at it; for me, it isn't natural. My brain is wired to look at the worst in situations instead of the best. I must directly counteract these thoughts, which is difficult, but I'm up for the challenge.

I reluctantly dragged myself to the doctor's office recently. I prayed, I pleaded, and I just felt like I wasn't getting any better. The doctor ordered a chest X-ray because my lungs didn't sound clear, then gave me a breathing treatment. Once she said 'X-ray,' my mind went to the worst place imaginable.

Then, from somewhere deep inside, a voice said, "Do you trust yourself?"

My answer? "Yes."

My thought was that I have no choice. I panicked some, then gave in. I said, "I know things will only get better."

The doctor came in and said my X-ray was clear, listened to my chest again, and said the treatment helped. She gave me some medicine and sent me on my way.

Visualization

There was a day when I visualized myself completing a book. I saw myself helping others with panic, and I saw the book completed. I imagined not having to worry about finances, and a sense of peace swept over me.

The strangest thing happened today. I focused on others. The same day, my bank statement revealed a balance that I didn't expect. My brother texted me and told me he had the money from last month to pay me back, all of which I had forgotten about.

A coincidence? Yes.

Could I also be manifesting?

Yes.

It's better to try than not to try at all. I felt a flow of inner peace today.

At lunchtime, my husband came home. He looked disheveled, and I smelled alcohol. Normally, I would question him, yell at him, and feel panic and fear. This time, I told him I loved him.

I hugged him, and said, "I know you're trying hard, thank you." I said a prayer for him that he'd find his way and went about my day with peace and calm. I don't know where it's coming from, but I choose peace and harmony any day over fear and anxiety or panic attacks. I can pray and offer support to others, but I will never be able to truly fix, change, or heal another person. They have that power and must find it within themselves.

While in the steam room today after a workout, I noticed a funny smell that was neither bad nor good. It made my eyes water a little. Just then a man said to another man, "I put eucalyptus oil on the outside of that hose so it will vapor out and clear my sinuses."

Then he proceeded to say that it could be a skin irritant; if you put it directly on your skin and if you ingest it, it could kill you. I left, and my mind started going to the place of, "Your throat is itchy, and even if you can't ingest it, I'm sure inhaling it is bad too."

I stopped my negative thoughts from their onset. I wiped them like an eraser board and said to myself, "You're not going there. If it turns out it is making you sick, you'll go see a doctor, but right now, you are perfectly okay. Don't give yourself a reason to go into a panic."

As quick as the scary thoughts came, they left quickly as well, and I was able to resume my day in peace.

I mowed my elderly neighbor's lawn, and I didn't have to, but good things manifested, and I didn't expect it. Sometimes the Universe is quick to reward, sometimes it takes its time, but it knows.

I went out today, and the negative thoughts were bombarding my mind. It's a constant struggle for me to keep the feelings of lack, feelings of inadequacy, and feelings of being unsafe and unprotected away.

Before, I would have had a full-fledged panic attack, and I'd be running to my apartment for comfort and the cycle would keep repeating. I long for the times of freedom when I was able to travel anywhere, by myself or with others. When I could meet a stranger, go to new places, and have no doubts. I long for deep connections. I want to have a deep connection, to be fully accepted, and completely loved.

Moving Forward

There were days when I had the answers, the keys to my inner confidence, the keys that opened my world. When I went to Puerto Vallarta, I went diving, paragliding, and bungee jumping, and had no fear. I didn't do these things to show off, I enjoyed the challenges, the adventure.

I am writing full time and keeping the house kept up along with daily cooking. I can add being a basketball coach to the list. It doesn't seem like much, but it keeps me busy from 8:00 a.m. until I fall asleep.

Panic attacks robbed me of some essential years of my life. I missed out on parties, gatherings, weddings, baby showers, and numerous other social occasions. I made up excuse after excuse so I wouldn't have to deal with the physical symptoms of panic. I tried to avoid the sweating, dizziness, rapid breathing, and the general feeling of dying. I used to think it mostly had to do with my dad's passing. As I evaluate my life, I know it has so much more to do with not being okay with uncertainty, such as my mortality, the well-being of my son, and the fear of becoming helpless.

I stop myself in moments of panic and ask, "Is this thought really true?" I break my thought process down by using Byron Katie's "The Work."

My answer is always a resonant, "No." At this moment my son and I are perfectly fine. It's my irrational thinking causing the mental torture, which then manifests into physical symptoms. Even if a bad situation is true, I can put my faith in myself, so that I will know how to react and handle myself. When I come to this conclusion, the intense fear leaves as fast as it comes.

When I rationalize like this to myself, I can finally stop panic in its tracks. A breakthrough! It's much easier to write and move on with the day when things in my mind are simple and perfect, even though I know perfect days won't last forever.

A scary thing happened to me; I had a bad sinus infection. There was fluid in my ears. When I flicked my head forward to dry my hair, my world went spinning. I made it to my bedroom and lay still on the bed. I lay there watching the ceiling spin. My mind was telling me, "There has to be a reason for this, and it's treatable."

Then my panic-ridden mind intervened and said, "You're dying! This is not normal."

I laid there until the spinning subsided. It seemed like hours but was a span of ten minutes. I immediately searched YouTube for a way to stop vertigo. I did the Epley maneuver technique, which eased the symptoms. I ended up going to the doctor and was told I had fluid in my ear along with a sinus infection. I was given antibiotics and told to rest. Lying still for two days straight gave me a lot of time to contemplate everything in life. I even had some deep dreams.

I had a dream where I was at an amusement park, and I had the choice between taking an easy boring slide, or a tall, scary, swirling slide that was next to it. I jumped forward on the scary one and zoomed down it. On the way down, I thought to myself, "Where has all my joy gone?" At the end of the slide, I was greeted by a bunch of smiling faces. It was Christmas time, and everyone was merry. I felt the warmth and giving of Christmas and thought to myself, "I'm still capable of feeling joy; it's a matter of being able to manifest it more often."

Setbacks are difficult to rebound from. Some people can have the same symptoms as I did with vertigo and be out jogging the next day. If they happen to fall over dizzy, they can move forward and are unfazed. I, however, feel the need to fix the problem right away. To me, going jogging and getting hurt even worse means I would not be the best mom I could be to my son.

Then there is the part of me that is self-conscious. I feel like if I fell over walking, I'd die of embarrassment. I know where this self-consciousness stems from. My mom would always tell me, "Don't do that, don't make yourself look stupid, they may laugh at you."

She may have been well-meaning at the time, but hearing the words was such a blow to my self-esteem. Feelings of always being judged, of not wanting to disappoint, not wanting to fail…sometimes, I find myself pushing these tendencies onto my son, but I stop, and I tell myself, "He is your son, trust him enough to let him make his own choices."

It is a conscious effort, but one I must keep practicing.

Who am I? I am broken, but still fixable. I can be as calm as a stream, as loving as a newborn puppy, and curious like a three-year-old child. I am all these things and more.

In my heart, I know these health issues will subside. I need to make the most of what I can do. I must heal my inner child and her past feelings of abandonment and rejection, heal the idea of not being good enough and not feeling safe. I need to embrace the feeling, "You did your best today; you made your best effort."

In the past, I have spent a lifetime chasing after things I thought I needed. I wanted to be in the presence of people whom I thought were more dignified, smarter, and a step above everyone else. I wanted some of their glory to rub off on me. Meanwhile, I overlooked the ones who stood by me through rough times.

In college, it was the elusive people that intrigued me, professors, and the anchors at the television station I worked at. It was difficult to maintain a friendship with them, yet I tried so hard to fit in with them. I am now thankful for their rejection, happy that I didn't fall into a pattern of befriending others for my own gain.

All the people I've encountered on my journey I have not met by accident. They were put into my life to teach me lessons, test my patience, and encourage and challenge me. People in my life are meant to be here, whether I feel they serve me in a good way or not. They are here on this life journey with me, some for a moment, others for a lifetime, and they either become my greatest allies or a life lesson on what not to become. I prefer to look at anyone I encounter as an ally until proven otherwise. In today's world, it can be difficult to see the good in everyone. Most people truly do the best they can with the knowledge they have. I can honestly say through the decisions I have made up until now, I did the best I could.

When I look at an individual now, I look for their inner light, their sincerity, and integrity; that's what attracts me. Not the outward projection, but the inward one.

If you are reading this and are in a dark moment, if you are lost, I hope that my words will somehow reach you. My hope is this book can touch you, like a warm strong hug, holding you in your time of need. My message is never give up, we are all in this together. One day, you're going to see how incredible you are, and how the world can be a forgiving place. If you are in a storm right now, know that the sun will shine again, my friend. There is a light, there is a rainbow at the end of the storm. Be patient, be loving, have hope, and this soon shall pass. Just as a storm cannot last forever, grief and hopelessness cannot either. If you are struggling with a loss, with time you will find comfort.

Our loved ones are always present in the energy that surrounds us, especially if we hold on to an item that once belonged to them. For me, the object that emits my father's energy is his enormous dresser drawer. If I concentrate, I can feel his energy, which is strong, powerful, and honest. I smell the pine, and it creates a picture of him in my mind. At that point, it's as if I have called his presence forth, and he remains for seconds. You can hold on to an object of a loved one who has passed, and if you concentrate in silence, you can feel them come forth. It's beautiful.

Spiritual Connection

My cousin came over recently. He started telling me about how he was going through a rough time. I told him this story, the one I am telling you now, about searching for my path.

He looked at his watch and said, "It's 11:11 p.m. What does that mean?"

He burst into tears. "I was going to end my life last weekend. I think I was meant to be right here at this very moment with you. I finally believe there is something out there, greater than me."

At that moment, I knew my struggle was not much different than what most of us face. If

I can convince one person to start searching for their true inner essence and to embrace themselves, I've done what I've been sent here to do.

My husband and I are still married; my son and I stay with him on the weekends. We've had this arrangement for the past year, and the situation has had its ups and downs. I have my son to think of; he loves his dad, and he enjoys us being together as a family unit.

It's been working out because my husband has been working, coming home, and doing what I believe he's supposed to do. He's been playing with and helping my son with his homework. Intimacy has been hard because he's lost my trust.

Then today it happened; I found pills and a pipe on him. I wasn't startled, but all the old fears and suspicions came to the surface again.

An outsider looking in would say, "You

should leave him for good."

I told my husband that if someone I connected with came along, I'd explore outside our relationship. He didn't give me a response back.

I've prayed hard for my husband's sobriety. In the dream I had, I was running through a maze, and I'd reached the end. I saw my husband; he was lost in the maze too. He was trying to find me, then he found me and ran toward me.

"I'm still here, I just took a different path," he said.

Today, he apologized and said, "I understand why you don't trust me. I'm sorry, this relapse makes me realize how everything could be gone in an instant, and I'm ashamed."

Then he wrote down a simple family rule to follow and pinned it on the refrigerator. "We are here to uplift one another."

In my heart, all my emotions—the distrust, sadness, anger, and hopelessness—have come up. Now I know this is on him, he has a choice, it's his life, his fight. I'm here for him, but I'm not doing his footwork. I know he doesn't want to be an addict; I know he wants something better. I'm not sure what he'll choose to do.

For now, I keep my heart guarded. I choose to still be with him on a part-time basis; that's my choice. I know he's hurt me, but deep within, I know that we still have things to learn from each other and that our soul contract isn't up. When times are going well, everything flows effortlessly. In difficult times, it feels as though the world is falling apart. I choose to stay with him for now, and I want him to beat his addiction.

For the first time, I have aspirations to travel, explore, get out in life, meet new people…even a new partner. I have isolated myself by the habits I have formed, habits meant to keep me safe, yet these habits have set me back. There is more to life than being careful and calculated. I want that part of myself back that was fearless, that had no limits, that was carefree and spontaneous. I lost her, and I'm searching for her again.

I took a self-inventory and found out I am failing badly. It's been so hard to dig deep and look at all my shortcomings. For instance, I have fallen. I have fallen so far, I now shake my head and wonder, how did that happen? My focus has been scattered and skewed. I've been focused on my phone, on social media, on sports, auto racing, and some of the wrong people.

I tend to chase after people who ignore me or they put me last when I put them first. I must like the challenge; I bend over backward for them, and inside, I want them to accept and like me. All the while, others are waving and bending over backward for my attention, and I don't give back to them like I know I should.

I am consciously aware now, and it's time for a change.

I did something that made me feel silly today. Remember the podcast that said to record yourself as though you'd already accomplished your goal? Today I sat with my recorder on my phone, and I put myself in a state of abundance. I talked into the recorder as though I had already accomplished my goals. I heard, for the first time, a tone of happiness and confidence.

I felt it!

I said, "I am an author, I travel, I visit people, and we talk about things that uplift us. I am financially stable, I am 'anxiety' free, and I am happy." When I finished recording and listened to it, it felt real. I will be listening to this daily, and I will make new recordings.

Power

I was sitting under a rickety, tattered, old white roller coaster. I was fenced off in a yard with the out of order roller coaster towering above me. I looked at the roller coaster and thought of the joy that it once had for others. I was in dreamland, and it was colorful and gave me a sense of nostalgia. The roller coaster was a metaphor for my life; it had many ups and many downs, joy and terror, happiness, and sadness. I looked ahead and saw a yard. and beyond the yard was an open road. To me the road represented freedom and infinite possibilities. My immediate intuition told me that I needed to get to the open road. I hopped on top of the fence and looked into the yard that I needed to pass in order to get to the road. Inside the yard was a large white tiger with vague black stripes on it. It was majestic, powerful, and ready to pounce. I didn't care, I was trapped and unhappy. I took a leap of faith and jumped into the yard with the majestic beast. I noticed a firestick, one like my grandmother kept at her house. I picked up the stick as the tiger came walking toward me; I held the stick up in front of my face, waiting to be pounced upon. Instead, the tiger looked at me and walked the other way. I ran to the other side of the yard and jumped on the fence and hopped on to the road. "I am free and fearless," came to mind.

The Shift

I know my mind is powerful and that it can work for or against me.

I've worked on projection by visualizing what I want as though I already have it. It's been difficult, especially when it comes to doubts, fears, and anxiety. My mind has a way of feeding into that and making it real. I literally must talk myself down or out of a panic attack because my mind goes to a deep, dark place where everything is a struggle.

Panic attacks are still prevalent, and they may be a constant part of my life; still, they are exhausting and suck the life out of me. I am learning to accept them when they come, rather than fighting it, and the attacks seem to be subsiding quicker.

Of course, my main goal is to never have them again, to obliterate them out of my sphere. However, for now, the goal is to get through them as quickly as they come. I have been able to cut the time of a panic attack in half.

Usually, they last ten to fifteen minutes, which doesn't seem very long. However, when you can't seem to breathe right and your mouth is dry and you're incoherent, minutes seem like hours.

Now, I've been able to say, okay, go ahead, come about; sometimes it manifests for a short time, and sometimes it doesn't even come. That's progress, and as long as I'm moving somewhere, I'm happy about the progress.

What may seem like frivolous steps have been major steps for me. I have been attending crowded places and forcing myself to shop in the back of big stores. It's uncomfortable at first, but I've been retraining my mind to think of pleasant things, and it's working. I think the key for me is to stop avoiding unpleasant situations. To endure them and talk to myself as I would to a good friend who is having a difficult time.

I am getting comfortable with doing things by myself, I see my alone time as a time for opportunity. I used to be attached at the hip to my husband, now I am alone a lot and I approach my situation as a new freedom, instead of lack.

What is missing today is human compassion and empathy. I was thinking about my circumstances; I am doing okay, not great, not bad, but okay. I was born into a middle-class family and had a good childhood.

"What if I'd been abused, gone hungry, and witnessed domestic violence daily?" I'd probably be angry and would have dropped out of school.

Also, on the flip side, what if my family had been wealthy, and I was able to attend private school and an Ivy League college? Would I be a doctor? Would I be a scholarly writer? Would I have succumbed to the high pressures of perfection?

What I do know is that I could be anyone out there, from the homeless lady to the actress or the brain surgeon. We are more alike and connected than we know, yet people distinguish themselves as being different, and it creates a divide.

As I sit here, I have memories. Two years ago, all three of my uncles were alive. I feel fortunate, though, that I always gave them hugs and told them how special they were to me. I remember standing outside with my uncle Junior, three months before he passed, and saying, "Uncle, I'm so glad you are here. I want you to know you will always hold a special place in my heart." He smiled.

I had heart-to-heart talks, whether in person or over the phone, with all three of my uncles who have passed and a cousin who was my brother. I had no idea at the time that I would lose them so quickly. They did their jobs here on Earth, and they made an imprint on my heart.

My uncle Tom made me aware of my intellect; my uncle Junior made me proud to be compassionate toward others. My cousin Hank brought laughter into the world. My uncle Alex made me realize that one's spirit never leaves those they love; there are never goodbyes. My dad made me realize that with hard work, effort, and a never give up attitude, you can create your own miracles.

As I started to shift and develop a deep love for myself, something happened.

I went to a restaurant with a girlfriend. We talked for hours about auras, UFOs, sex, our aspirations, dreams, and childhood traumas. For the first time, there was a sense that my bare soul was being seen. At the end of our dinner, we stared into each other's eyes, and it felt like I could venture into her soul. As we walked outside, we embraced for a minute; there was a spark that I hadn't felt in a long time. I felt like I was home. She confirmed to me later in a phone call that the feeling of attraction was mutual.

My love for her reminded me of the time I read Plato's "Symposium." Diotima described love best as: "We are attracted to the beauty within that person."

For now, I need to keep working on myself as a human being. I am not able to start a new relationship. However, it's invigorating and empowering to discover that love is all around me and is abundant within many forms. I discovered within myself a new awareness and a new definition of how love can be defined for me.

FINDING MY SACRED

I released an old paradigm that I was holding on to about the definition of love. That release has brought an expansiveness to my world, and it is healing.

Indianapolis 500

If you had asked me a year ago if I ever thought I would attend the Indianapolis 500, I would have called you crazy. Susan, a friend of mine in Michigan, bought our tickets (I would be going with my cousin), and my first instinct was to immediately back out. I racked my brain with everything from "I can't get off work" to "My son has an important basketball tournament."

Yes, I had a habit of lying to get out of important events. But on this day, it came to a stop. I would no longer enable myself. I was ashamed of my condition for too long, and now it's out in the open. I have told people about my battle; I have revealed a part of who I am.

I ran through the list of why I shouldn't go, and you know what? My list of why I *should go* outweighed my list of why I shouldn't go. Without overthinking it, my flight to Indianapolis, Indiana, was booked. If I had waited for the perfect moment, it would have never come to fruition.

Finally, I was okay with it; it would be an opportunity of a lifetime.

I thought of myself as being old; if I didn't go, it would be something that would haunt me forever. I knew deep inside if I didn't fight my inner demons, I would never experience the beauty of life. I spent thirteen years in my own prison, and I didn't need to give myself a life sentence.

When I decided to go to Indianapolis, it gave me a sense of freedom and pride that I hadn't felt in years. For the first time, I felt I could really do it! For the first time, I believed it was possible to travel to Italy and see the Sistine Chapel, the Colosseum, and more places. For the first time, I believed I could accomplish impossible tasks. I had my keys; I could open new doors and experience all that life had to offer. Or I could remain in my comfort zone and keep the doors locked and live with the unhappy mental blocks that kept me trapped.

For most people, a trip to the Indianapolis 500 would be an instant dream come true. For someone crippled with anxiety like me, I had to talk myself up.

On my way home from a basketball game, I had the onset of a panic attack. I was coming home, and it was late, and I made a wrong turn and the thought "We are lost" came to mind. My mind started racing, and I had to talk myself down.

"Look, you found the road again," I had to tell myself.

"Look, that store is familiar." The panic stopped in its tracks.

The immediate thought of "You will know nobody, and you won't recognize a damn thing in Indianapolis" came to my mind. Then the worry came about how I was going to cope with the unfamiliarity. The massive crowds?

Because of my apprehension, I scheduled some counseling sessions with a therapist. I asked my doctor for anti-anxiety medication for the plane trip going there and coming back. I had traveled on a plane before, yet it was years before I started having panic attacks. I set up two plans of action for the plane ride there and back.

Watch the movie *Superbad* on the way there, and coming home, sleep the entire way.

When I left for Indianapolis, I took the lowest dose of Xanax possible and headed out the door. It had been years since I'd taken

Xanax. I popped a pill and was dropped off at the airport. I had two carry-on bags and headed upstairs through security. All my negative thoughts rushed at me all at once! The first was, "Look at that line, it will take forever to get through it!"

I counteracted it with, "I'm going and will wait like everyone else is doing."

Ten minutes into waiting, my mom called. I talked to her for as long as I could, then she said she had to go.

The thought "You're trapped" popped into my head. The physical symptoms began to onset; I drank my water.

"If you turn back now," I told myself, "You'll have to live with this failure until you're old and gray, and you'll never forgive yourself."

A part of me wanted to run out of the line and bolt home. I stood there with a dry mouth, feeling hot. I remained in line and tried to distract myself. I told myself, "This is your dream trip, you've got this." I looked for an object as a distraction. I saw a clock. I started to describe the clock in my head. It worked for a few minutes.

I remained in the line and finally made it through security. I saw my cousin, Cody, who was there to meet me. He immediately greeted me and gave me a big hug. I gathered myself as we walked to the boarding area. I headed to the restroom, took another Xanax, and splashed my face with water. I gave myself a pep talk. I walked out and I felt calmer. My plane was boarding.

We boarded the plane, and I filled my head with thoughts of already being in Indianapolis, of seeing the race cars. I sat calmly in my seat. Surprisingly, it was like sitting in any other chair. I buckled myself in and we took off. I started my movie, *Superbad*, and then, before too long, we landed in Indiana!

When I walked into the overwhelmingly large Indy airport, I didn't know which way to go, and immediately my heart raced. But I told myself to breathe slowly. I bought a soda and started sipping it; I distracted myself by taking in all the colors, all the sights, all the sounds. Soon my cousin Cody and I were by the exit, and déjà vu occurred. This was the dream before my car accident! This was the dream where I am in a room with people who can't move. In my dream, I must force myself out of the room and crawl with all my might, until I finally reach the door. I open it and start limping out of the room. I put on a mask and limp to the exit; I reach the exit, and throw off my mask, and am well again.

As I stood, overlooking the exit; it looked exactly like the scene in my dream: the large windows, the colors, the energy! "I am having déjà vu," I tell Cody. "I've seen this scene vividly before in my dream."

He says, "It's a good sign. It means you're on the right path and you recognize it."

We walked outside the airport. We found my friend waiting for us. I hugged her, and we drove to the guest house. I felt normal. No nerves! My dream was coming true.

I walked around the property and neighborhood in peace. "Thank you, Creator," I said.

The trip turned out to be amazing. I saw the track, the pagoda, and Indy cars zooming around the oval. It seemed like a dream; it was hot, but I was in Indy! I saw the garages and my favorite race car drivers up close. My favorite moment was when I woke up early one morning and saw a squirrel in a tree next to me, and I loved looking at the stars at night.

Authentic Self

I think first and foremost, to find me, I needed to find my unique purpose and what my inner drive was. What was I passionate about? For me, it was writing and basketball. What am I willing to do right now to take small steps toward making my passions a reality? Who could I surround myself with or tap into to assist me with getting my accomplishments off the ground?

I visualized an author to mentor me. I wrote to numerous authors and…nothing. I then committed to four hours of writing each day, rain or shine, sick or healthy, four hours, Monday through Friday. I also visualized myself writing in an office and treating it like a job. My mind wanted to go to a place of lack, and through practice, I counteracted it by seeing myself with abundance. I told myself I will write books, and I will continue coaching basketball. Instead of buying coffee, instead of going to the movies, I will spend the little savings I have accumulated on self-improvement classes.

At one point, I was addicted to my electronic devices. There was a time I used my social media account as my only means of social interaction. It is a good way to communicate with friends, family, and even strangers when done occasionally. However, it was a detriment to me because it was becoming my only means of interaction. I now limited myself to an hour on the internet. The reason being, the internet is filled with misinformation and persuasive ideologies, and it divides us as a species. I have turned off all the alarms and ringers on my phone, which allowed me to free up a lot of my time, which is now used for writing and exercising. It was difficult at first because I felt like I was missing out, but now I can say it's been liberating. It's liberating to have absolute control of my thoughts, instead of outside influences and messages persuading me to be thinner, wiser, richer, etc.

After this life, nobody will remember the small details of me spilling coffee on my shirt, not ironing my clothes, or having frumpy hair. People will remember if I was there for them and how I made them feel when I was in their presence. I will either leave a good or bad memorable imprint with them.

Deep inside, I've always felt like a writer. I thought I needed a role model, a compassionate and creative Navajo woman like me to look up to. Little did I know, her presence was already there.

I've learned in life, the answers we seek are always much closer than we realize.

With the assistance of some self-improvement classes, I have become laser focused on who I am. I know who I am now. *I am a powerful, creative, loving woman of light. My purpose is connection, empowerment, and spirituality. I create healing, truth, compassion, and knowing in the world. I assist men and women with extreme anxiety in finding their unique spiritual path and living their true authentic selves.*

Finding My Sacred

I started writing this book in 2011. You have followed me through my journey of overcoming panic and anxiety. It's eleven years later, and I have to say with exuberance, I no longer take medication and I no longer have panic attacks! I still get nervous, however; I am aware that being nervous now means that I care about the outcome of the endeavor. Being nervous is a part of being human, being nervous is okay, but letting my nerves run away with me is not. Now, looking back, I know without realizing it, I trained my brain to go into panic mode.

By listening to teachers like Wayne Dyer, Byron Katie, Mel Robbins, Deepak Chopra, Eckhart Tolle, and my grandmother Sue, I was able to meditate and turn my thoughts around. Along with exercise and my therapist, Sallee, I was able to overcome agoraphobia, panic attacks, and feelings of abandonment.

I took Impact Training classes and was able to transform from a dependent, needy daddy's girl into an independent grown-up who will always love her father. And yet, I know I am his grown adult child. I have my own resources; I have my own back. It's not my father's job to watch over me; I need to watch over myself, and I am fully capable.

Around Thanksgiving, fall of 2020, I visited a neighbor who was 90 years old; his name was Bob Clements. He was a professional dancer and a psychic channeler. He told me he quit psychic channeling because he could no longer physically do it without feeling exhausted. I never asked for a psychic reading from him because of his fragile state.

My mom had me deliver some soup to him and his wife.

On my way, I put on my earphones and listened to a random YouTube song, "Heal Your Soul, Ancestral Chants from the Native Americans."

If you have access, please stop and put this song on, then finish reading this with the song playing.

The song reminds me of both my *shicheii* and *shinálí*, Shank Tsosie and Nelson Smith, singing confidently to me as the fire flickers in their humble tiny hogans.

It reminds me of all the hardships my ancestors endured before me. No running water, no indoor plumbing, mistreatment at boarding schools, no doctors or pharmaceutical medications. They gathered plants and made their own teas and medicines. They relied on blessings and the faith that there was something greater than themselves guiding them. They butchered their own sheep and cows, grew their own vegetables, and lived off the land. I think of my strong grandma Sue, being a young girl, hiding in the rock caves with her family to escape the cavalry. Her parents were only armed with an unwavering will to survive and a selfless need to protect their children and the elderly.

When I walk through the doorway of Bob's eclectic, high vibrating, energetic house, his wife isn't there. I turn down my air pods and hand him the soup. His beautiful, weary, light blue eyes stare into my eyes; I sense he is reading me, and I stand in silence. I have complete trust in him.

He says, "There is a Native American lady, dressed all in white, she has turquoise jewelry on, and she is standing next to you."

I look around me and see nothing.

"She is making a hugging motion towards you," he quietly says. "She is motioning her hands down like she is staying put. I get the sense she is fiercely protective over you. She is with a little boy. Man, he's cute." Bob chuckles. "She's motioning, 'He's with me.' Do you know who she is? Who's the little boy?"

I instantly remember what the quantum healer once told me. I am overcome with emotions of overwhelming love; I can't hold it together. I quickly tell Bob thank you and exit out the door. I don't see anything. I look all around me, yet I sense her strong motherly presence in my heart. I sense the boy is my unborn baby; I feel his love and playfulness. They are together. I turn my air pods up again as the hypnotic flute plays.

I say out loud, "You're my biological mother, aren't you?"

A crow lands on the edge of Bob's fence, which I interpret as a yes.

As if on cue, a lady starts talking on my headphones. She is telling me how beautiful I am in Navajo. It's as if the Universe has conspired to give me this message from her at that precise moment.

The thought "I will never be alone again" comes to my mind.

Another thought, "You are forgiven for not having the unborn baby," pops into my head.

I think of the traveling fake priest who told me I was going to hell. His presence was a wake-up call to me. Not he, nor anyone else ever had any authority over my mind, body, and soul.

I called the diocese the day after he freaked out on me, and at the end of the week, they called me back and told me he had never been a real priest. They asked him to leave the church, and he was promptly gone. I didn't need his forgiveness anyway. I alone needed to forgive myself. I had done the best

I could amidst difficult circumstances. The fact that I was looking toward a stranger to validate and forgive me is nonsensical.

My heart is flowing with inner peace, and a weight seems to have been lifted from my shoulders. I have the biggest goofy smile on my face as I walk through the neighborhood. I want to hug everyone I encounter. I have the whimsical feeling of the ending of *It's a Wonderful Life*, my all-time favorite movie. This was my missing puzzle piece! What I had been searching for, outside of myself and from other people, had been found.

A woman, now an all-knowing soul who I interpreted as being my biological mother, had spoken to me. The truth was always within me; my once broken pieces are now whole again. I feel the presence of my biological mother beaming at me. She is proud of me and very protective. I close my eyes and envision a woman much like myself, only older.

Bittersweet tears roll down my cheeks, and the song ends. There are tears of sadness at never meeting her on this earthly realm and tears of relief for finally finding my sacred self.

No, my birth parents didn't give up on me or abandon me. They knew they couldn't provide me with the opportunities that I needed. Instead, they gifted me to two wonderful, loving parents that bestowed love and became my role models.

The moment I told myself, "You will never measure up," I gave my power away.

The moment I told myself, "Writing a book is impossible," I doused my own dreams.

The moment I said, "I can't live without my husband," I gave up on *me*.

As I think back to my dream about the majestic white tiger, I realize who that tiger symbolized. It was me! I was that strong presence; I was fearful of myself. Once I faced the fear and took the leap, although it was uncomfortable, it gave me confidence and freedom.

I was the one who abandoned me. Knowing this, I am now confident that I will never abandon myself again. I choose not to break my own heart, ever again!

My mother is aging; she's strong but fragile and depends on me now more than ever. She wants my company every day, if not in person, through a phone call. If I hadn't healed my soul, if I hadn't done the work, my demeanor today would be much different toward her. If I harbored feelings of anger and resentment, with an attitude of "How does it feel to be in my shoes now?" I would have remained angry and broken.

It makes me cringe to think of how hurt and fragile I was. Now I love both moms so much it hurts. I am grateful for being shown how to be strong and resilient. In a twist of fate, my mom, Ida, has become me, and I have now become her in a way.

I am now the flaming fire to be reckoned with, heaven help me. I am the one who makes dire decisions regarding our family. Without her, I wouldn't have recognized my strengths. Her tough love was what I needed, and it took me a long time to recognize and embrace it.

The crows I used to see daily are gone now. But they left a message: "Your father sent us because he knew you needed support. You don't need his support anymore because you found your own power."

Yes, I miss seeing them daily in the earthly realm, but I know they are thriving in the spiritual realm, and I am grateful for them.

I embrace the many seasons of my life that have come and gone. Currently, my days consist of meditating daily, writing daily, and connecting to Spirit. I've manifested an office, I've manifested the person of my dreams, and I've manifested abundance. I was broken, and I waited to be put back together. But unbeknownst to me, I was the only one who could put myself back together again. I was the lifeboat all along. I was the lone rescuer.

New messages are being delivered to me daily, and individuals who are healers are coming into my life. New stories are developing for me to tell; a rebirth is taking place.

Your existence at this exact time on Earth is not an accident. You are needed to heal this planet, to heal your inner soul, and to love yourself and humanity at the highest level possible. This world is beautiful and filled with infinite possibilities. Clarity, resolution, and beauty are within all of us. Surrender to unloading the hard stuff, and you will discover how to find *your* sacred. Many Blessings.

A'he'hee'

> # FINDING MY SACRED

Acknowledgements

If I was on an Oscar podium, this is what I would say: My journey of course started with my core family, my *shimá*, Ida Smith, and my *shizhé'é*, Richard Nelson Smith. My *shitsilí*, Darrick Smith, and my other furry brother, Benji.

Thank you for choosing me, Mom and Dad. You didn't have to, but you adopted us and raised us with all the integrity and love that you could give.

Next, the rock in our family, my beautiful grandmother Sue, you are pure love and light, you are who I aspire to be like. My auntie Lori and aunt Brenda, thank you for assisting with the photo shoot, lots of love to you both. My sis Sherlyn, I appreciate your presence.

To my partner and father of my child, Dan Darling. Life has handed you great obstacles.

The fact that you choose to fight every day is inspiring. Keep up the hard work.

To my extended family, uncles, aunties, cousins, nieces, and nephews, and my partner in crime, Jenn. I learn from all of you every day, and without you, this book could not be possible. I love you, thank you.

To my boys' basketball team: Thank you for all the good times!

To all my colleagues at World Systems Solutions, this is for you, Diversity Group. We can do it!

To all the brave souls who have taken on Impact Training classes, especially Lift Off 405 & 407, I love your light. Thank you, Marilyn.

My dear in-laws, thank you for being there: Debbie, Jim, and Sandy. You will forever be in my heart, Roger Wesley Simmons, your songs are "Starlight" and "Piano Man."

A special thanks to Julie Artz for guiding the

developmental edit and Rob Bignell for your accurate fact-checking. The final edit, Kristin Waller, thank you.

Also, thank you to Kathryn and Douglas Jones for making this manuscript a reality.

Finally, though not last, to my dear loving son (*shíyáázh*), Adante Quinn Darling, this is for you. I love you to the moon. You make this mama proud.

FINDING MY SACRED

Shell Silversmith completed her Bachelors of Arts in Family and Human Development from the University of Utah in 1995. She is Navajo and understands both Navajo and Spanish. She was awarded a fellowship to the Emerging Diné Writers' Institute in New Mexico, which she completed in 2022. She is on the diversity team at World Systems Solutions, a healing platform near and dear to her heart. Shell's purpose is to help others overcome agoraphobia and severe anxiety. She hopes you enjoy her journey and encourages everyone to find their sacred.

www.ingramcontent.com/pod-product-compliance
Lightning Source LLC
Chambersburg PA
CBHW070139100426
42743CB00013B/2763